Louisiana We're Really Cookin'! ™

GREAT FLAVORS OF LOUISIANA
*is dedicated to Louisiana cooking,
a true marriage of Cajun, Creole, French, and New
American Cuisine that produces flavors that not only
Louisianians but all those who enjoy outstanding food can
become passionate about!*

1

SOUTHERN FLAVORS PUBLICATIONS

P.O. Box 922

Pine Bluff, Arkansas 71613

Copyright pending

Southern Flavors, Inc.

All rights reserved.

First Edition October 1987
Second Printing August 1988 10,000

Please use the order form in the back of the book to order additional copies of GREAT FLAVORS OF LOUISIANA and/or GREAT FLAVORS OF MISSISSIPPI.

WATCH FOR OTHER PUBLICATIONS FROM SOUTHERN FLAVORS, INC.

ISBN 0-9618137-1-7

Type & Graphics set by T.G.S. of Arkansas, Pine Bluff

THE PERDUE COMPANY

USA

FOREWORD

John Folse, the renowned Cajun Chef, has said that the kitchen is a place to exchange ideas and share recipes and that it's all right there in the kitchen with the creative cook with the spoon in his/her hand. GREAT FLAVORS OF LOUISIANA brings to your kitchen that "sharing" of recipes and exchange of ideas that he is speaking about! We hope that you will relish these 220 (kitchen tested) recipes as much as we did the collecting, testing, selecting, and particularly, the tasting of them!! Each one, be it a Cajun, Creole, French, or New American recipe, provides you a great flavor of Louisiana!

We heartily thank Lillie Petit Gallagher, author of LOUISIANA KEEPSAKE, for the use of the marvelous Louisiana Expressions, peppered throughout our book, that offer philosophical flavors of Louisiana's people. We thank Louisiana's Office of Tourism, Department of Wildlife and Fisheries, Seafood Promotion Board, and Department of Agriculture for the invaluable assistance in providing material for the Louisiana Facts, Festivals, Notables, and Places that are sprinkled throughout the book. Special thanks go to Chef John Folse, owner of LAFITTE'S LANDING RESTAURANT in Donaldsonville, Ralph Brennan, owner of MR. B.'S BISTRO in New Orleans, Suzie David Stephens, author of NIBBLES COOKS CAJUN, Jane Breaux of MINTMERE PLANTATION in New Iberia, and the Junior Leagues of Baton Rouge (RIVER ROADS COOKBOOKS I and II) and Lake Charles (PIRATE'S PANTRY COOKBOOK)!!

Our last and very special thank you goes to all cooks represented in GREAT FLAVORS OF LOUISIANA for by sharing their favorite recipes with us they now go from our kitchen to yours!! GREAT FLAVORS provides a distinctive flavor of Louisiana to the non-native and is a marvelous memento for the Louisiana native and visitor of the grand times and glorious food that Louisiana offers!! We invite you to savor and enjoy!

Nancy McIntyre, Co-Editor	**Ellen Reynolds, Co-Editor**	**Jeanne Verlenden, Editor**
Alexandria, Louisiana	**Shreveport, Louisiana**	

SOUTHERN FLAVORS, INC.

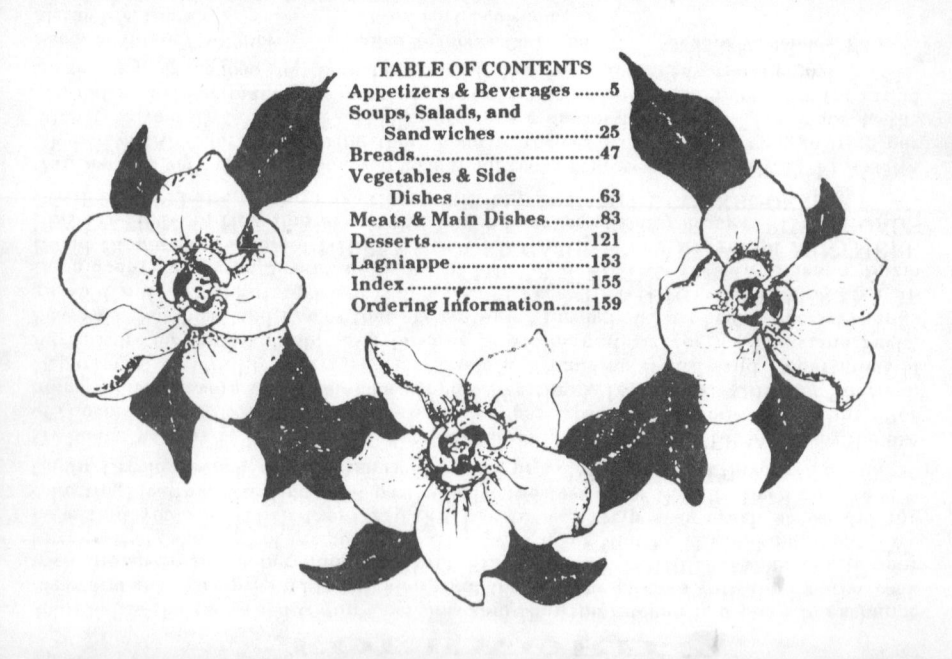

TABLE OF CONTENTS

APPETIZERS
AND
BEVERAGES

TOO GOOD ARTICHOKE DIP

1 (14 oz.) can artichoke hearts,
    drained and coarsely chopped
1 small onion, coarsely chopped

1 cup mayonnaise
1 pkg. dry Italian Salad
    Dressing Mix

Combine, and mix together well all ingredients. Refrigerate overnight. Serve with favorite crackers. Too good to be this easy!

SO GOOD BROCCOLI 'N CHEESE 'N CRAB MEAT DIP

1 (10 oz.) pkg. frozen chopped
    broccoli, cooked and drained
3 stems celery, finely chopped
1 medium onion, finely chopped
2 Tbsps. butter
1 can cream of mushroom soup

1 (6 oz.) roll garlic cheese
Worcestershire sauce to taste
Tabasco to taste
1/2 (10 oz.) can Rotel tomatoes,
    diced
2 (8 oz.) cans crab meat

Saute onion and celery in butter: add broccoli, soup, cheese, tomatoes, sauce, and Tabasco. Stir over medium heat until cheese melts. Stir in crab meat. Serve warm with crackers or melba rounds. LOUISIANA WONDERFUL!!!

Kathleen Drott, Pineville, Louisiana

LOUISIANA EXPRESSION:
Il n'y a pas de sauce qui egale l'appetit! THERE IS NO SAUCE LIKE APPETITE!!

SCRUMPTIOUS CRAB SPREAD

1 lb. crab meat
1/2 cup vegetable oil
1/2 cup vinegar

4-6 green onions, chopped, tops and all
Salt and pepper to taste

Combine all ingredients, and refrigerate overnight. Serve with favorite crackers. Yields 3 cups of pure delight!!

NEW ORLEANS CRAB MEAT CAVIAR

1 lb. crab meat
1/2 cup mayonnaise
1/2 cup chili sauce
1 avocado, thinly sliced
1 clove garlic, minced
Salt and pepper to taste

1 can (8 oz.) pitted black olives, finely chopped
1/2 cup sour cream
2 Tbsps. parsley, chopped
Fresh lemon juice to taste

Toss all ingredients together well. Serve with crackers. DELICIOUS!!

Suzie Stephens, Native of New Orleans, Louisiana
Author of NIBBLES COOKS CAJUN

LOUISIANA FACT:
New Orleans was founded in 1718 by de Bienville and within three years had a population of 400!

WONDERFUL GARLIC CHEESE BALL

2 (8 oz.) pkgs. cream cheese,
   softened
1 stick butter, softened
2½-3½ cloves garlic, crushed

1 bunch green onions, finely
   chopped, tops and all
2 Tbsps. parsley, chopped
1 cup pecans, chopped

Mix all ingredients together well. Shape into a ball. Chill several hours or overnight. Garnish with parsley, and serve with Ritz, rye, and sesame crackers, and melba rounds. Pretty served at Christmas using holly leaves as garnish! TRULY WONDERFUL!!

VAL DENLEY'S CHEESE LUMPS

1 (8 oz.) pkg. Kraft coon cheese
1 stick butter
4 egg whites, beaten stiff

1½ loaves French bread, crust
   removed

Melt butter and cheese together, blending well. Mix egg whites with cheese mixture. Tear bread into bite sized lumps. Dip bread into hot cheese. Then, enjoy!!
Yields 4-5 dozen.

Lucie Lee Lanoux, Alexandria, Louisiana

LOUISIANA PLACE:
Alexandria's Hotel Bentley was completed in 1908 and called the "Waldorf on the Red River" because of its lovely decor, marvelous food, and Southern hospitality. The Bentley, restored to its former grandeur and reopened in 1985, covers an entire city block.

8

AUNT CALLIE'S MARVELOUS CHEESE ROLL-UP

1 lb. Velveeta cheese (room temperature)
1 (8 oz.) pkg. cream cheese
1/2 cup Hellmann's mayonnaise
Juice of a lemon
1 medium bud garlic, chopped
3 green onions, chopped
10 or more ripe olives, chopped
Tabasco to taste
Lea & Perrins to taste
1/4 cup parsley, finely chopped
Paprika

Spread cheese on waxed paper. Mix next 8 ingredients; with this mixture, form a long round roll on top of cheese like a jelly roll. Wrap cheese around filling; chill. Before serving, roll in parsley and paprika. Serve sliced in rounds or on crackers.

JEZEBEL SAUCE

1 (18 oz.) jar pineapple preserves
1 (18 oz.) jar apple jelly
1 (6 oz.) jar dry mustard
1 (4 oz.) jar cream of horseradish
1 Tbsp. coarse ground pepper
1 (8 oz.) pkg. cream cheese

Combine first 5 ingredients, mixing well. Pour a generous amount of sauce over cream cheese. Serve with an assortment of crackers.
Yields 1 1/2 quarts.

Martha Andre, Native of Tallulah, Louisiana

LOUISIANA FACT:
On April 30, 1812, Louisiana became the 18th state admitted to the United States. At that time, New Orleans was Louisiana's capital. In 1882, Baton Rouge replaced New Orleans as the state capital.

9

MARVELOUS CLAM DIP "PENNY"

1 stick butter
3 Tbsps. onion, chopped
1 (6 1/2 oz.) can clams, drained and minced

1 (8 oz.) pkg. cream cheese
Several drops Tabasco
Dash of Lea and Perrins

In top of double boiler, saute onion in butter for 30 minutes. Add clams; saute for 30 minutes more. Add last 3 ingredients, mixing well. If mixture separates, add a few drops of water, and blend. Serve hot in chafing dish. This dip is wonderful served with steamed artichokes, your favorite crackers, or chips! Easily doubled.

Mary Kurzweg, Metairie, Louisiana

SHRIMP PATTY DO

1 (8 oz.) pkg. cream cheese, softened to room temperature
1/2 pt. sour cream
2 lbs. shrimp, cooked and shelled, (If shrimp are large, cut in half. Otherwise leave shrimp whole.)

3 green onions, tops and all, chopped
1/3 cup fresh parsley, chopped
Dash of Worcestershire sauce
Red pepper to taste

Mix together well all ingredients. Garnish with additional parsley sprigs. Serve in a clear glass bowl with sesame seed crackers. This dip is marvelous, pretty, and your family or guests will love it and you!!!

Mag Wall, Baton Rouge, Louisiana

LOUISIANA FACT:
Louisiana ranks first in natural gas production in the United States.

1½ cups tomato soup
1 (8 oz.) pkg. cream cheese
¼ tsp. salt
1 Tbsp. onion juice
Tabasco to taste
Lemon juice to taste
1¼ pkgs. gelatin
¼ cup cold water
½ cup mayonnaise

1 cup bell pepper, chopped
¼ cup celery, chopped
½ cup stuffed olives, sliced
2 Tbsps. pimento
2 cups crawfish, cooked and chopped
1 cup crab meat
½ cup whipping cream, whipped

Heat soup in top of double boiler. Add next 5 ingredients; heat until cheese softens, stirring frequently. Soften gelatin in cold water. Add gelatin to hot mixture; stir until dissolved. Cool. Add next 7 ingredients, mixing well. Fold in whipped cream; turn into a large mold that has been sprayed with Pam. Chill until firm. Serve with your favorite crackers. SO GOOD! May substitute shrimp for crawfish. Very pretty made in a crawfish mold! The mousse is also wonderful served as a salad on a bed of lettuce!

Compliments of Louisiana's Seafood Promotion and Marketing Board

LOUISIANA FACT:
The Acadians (or Cajuns) of South Louisiana (Acadiana) are best known for their friendliness, strong family ties, and their love and zest for life! The distinctive foods of Acadiana include gumbo, boudin, crawfish etouffee, sauce piquante, and jambalaya.

11

LOUISIANA SHRIMP 'N VEGETABLE MARINADE

3-5 lbs. shrimp, cooked, shelled, and
    cleaned
2 (8 1/2 oz.) cans artichoke hearts

1/2 lb. fresh mushrooms, halved
1 pt. cherry tomatoes, cleaned
Tarragon Marinade

Combine first 4 ingredients together in an air tight container. Add marinade (recipe below), cover tightly, and chill overnight. Drain before serving. Pretty served in a large glass bowl with toothpicks for scooping up shrimp and vegetables. Marvelous! Easily doubled.
Serves 24-30.

TARRAGON MARINADE

1 1/2 cups tarragon vinegar
1 medium onion, quartered
2 Tbsps. garlic, crushed
1 Tbsp. lemon juice
1 tsp. brown sugar

1 tsp. salad herbs
1/4 tsp. prepared mustard
Salt and pepper to taste
4 cups salad oil
1 cup olive oil

In a blender, combine first 8 ingredients for 5 seconds. Add oils, mixing until well blended.
Yields 6 1/2 cups.

Nina Long, Alexandria, Louisiana

HOT CHEESE PUFFS

4 ozs. cream cheese
3/4 tsp. onions, grated
1/4 cup Hellmann's mayonnaise
1 Tbsp. chives, chopped
1/8 tsp. cayenne pepper
1/8 cup Parmesan cheese
1/2 small loaf bread, 8 slices, crusts removed
Fresh parsley snips for garnish

In a bowl, combine the first 6 ingredients, mixing together well. Using a small round cookie cutter, cut 4 rounds from each slice of bread. Generously, spread each round with cheese mixture. Bake in a 350° oven for 15 minutes. This recipe is easily doubled, can be prepared up to 2 weeks in advance, and frozen (uncooked). The cooked puffs look so nice arranged on a tray and garnished with parsley! THE BEST AND EASIEST CHEESE PUFFS EVER!!

Susan Bee McNamara, Native of New Orleans, Louisiana

LOUISIANA NOTABLE:
The great Louis Armstrong was born in New Orleans on July 4, 1900. As a child, he loved jazz music and had a music group that "sang for its supper" on the streets of New Orleans. Armstrong, affectionately known as the great "Satchmo," was a superb jazz musician who played the trumpet and sang in movies and on radio and television.

JULIANNE'S TWO CHEESES PUFFS

1 cup water
1 stick butter
1 cup all purpose flour
1 1/2 tsps. salt
1/2 tsp. coarsely cracked pepper
4 eggs, room temperature

3/4 cup Gruyere cheese, firmly packed and grated
3/4 cup Parmesan cheese, freshly grated
Vegetable oil (for deep frying)

In heavy medium saucepan, combine water and butter; bring to a boil, and remove from heat. Add next 3 ingredients; beat with wooden spoon until incorporated. Set over medium heat, beating until mixture pulls away from sides of pan. Transfer dough to large bowl. Using electric mixer, beat in eggs, 1 at a time. Beat in cheeses. Heat oil in deep fryer (or skillet) until very hot (350°). Drop cheese mixture into oil by rounded teaspoonfuls (in batches and not crowding); fry until golden brown, 3-4 minutes. Remove with slotted spoon; drain on paper towels. Serve immediately. DELICIOUS AND UNIQUE!!
Yields about 60 delectable puffs!!

Julianne Lansing, New Orleans, Louisiana

LOUISIANA FACT:
New Orleans is unique among Louisiana and American cities. European visitors often comment that New Orleans is the only American city that resembles their own cities! This is, in large part, due to the Vieux Carre Historic District (French Quarter) which contains hundreds of distinctive buildings with lovely balconies.

14

DEVILED HAM PUFFS

1 (8 oz.) pkg. Philadelphia Cream
  Cheese
1 egg yolk, beaten well
1 tsp. onion juice
1/2 tsp. baking powder
1/2 tsp. salt

2 tsps. horseradish
1/4 tsp. Tabasco
Small bread rounds, 1-1 1/4 inch
  diameter, toasted lightly
1 (5 oz.) can deviled ham

Blend together well first 7 ingredients. Spread each toasted round with thin layer of deviled ham. Place cheese mixture in pastry bag with large star tip, and garnish each round with a rosette of cheese mixture. Place on cookie sheet; bake at 375° for 5–10 minutes until cheese is puffed and lightly browned.
Yields 75 marvelous puffs!

"These can be made ahead, and frozen on a cookie sheet before baking. When needed, thaw, bake, and hope you have enough! I baked 600 of these as appetizers for a son's rehearsal dinner. We had 110 guests, and no ham puffs left over!!"

                                    Kathleen Drott, Pineville, Louisiana

LOUISIANA FACT:
The highest point in Louisiana is Driskill Mountain which is 535 feet above sea level, and the lowest point is 5 feet below sea level in New Orleans!

DELICIOUS LITTLE MEAT PIES

1½ lbs. lean ground beef (Chuck or round is best!)
1 bell pepper, chopped
Red pepper to taste
Lemon pepper to taste

1 can mushroom soup
3 medium onions, chopped
6 cloves, garlic, minced
2 eggs

Brown meat; add remaining ingredients, excluding soup and eggs. Cook until done. Add soup and raw eggs, mixing well. Cool meat mixture; chill. Spoon 1 iced teaspoonful into each biscuit dough. Fold dough over meat filling, and seal with fork tines. Bake at 350° until biscuits are lightly brown, about 15-20 minutes. Pies may be frozen on cookie sheets and stored in freezer bags until needed.
Makes about 60 little pies.

CREAM CHEESE BISCUITS

3 sticks margarine, softened
3 (8 oz.) pkgs. cream cheese, softened

3 cups flour
½ iced teaspoonful red pepper

Mix together well margarine and cheese. Gradually, add flour and pepper, mixing together well. Roll out dough, and cut with biscuit cutter. **BISCUITS ARE WONDERFUL ALONE!!** (If you just make the biscuits, bake at 400° for 12-15 minutes, or until golden brown. Serve with butter and honey.)

Josie Gleason, Baton Rouge, Louisiana

AUNT CORA'S 14-DAY PICKLES

2 gals. cucumbers, sliced in horizontal slices (Do not peel!)
2 cups non-iodized salt
1 gal. boiling water
1 tsp. alum

FOR PICKLING MIXTURE:
5 pts. vinegar, boiling hot
6 cups sugar
1/2 oz. celery seed
1 cinnamon stick

Day 1: Put cucumbers in big crock. Dissolve salt in water; pour over cucumbers. Cucumbers must be immersed. (Use bowl to weight down cucumbers.) Let stand for 7 days. DAY 8: Drain; then, pour a gallon boiling water over cucumbers; let stand 24 hours. DAY 9: Drain; pour a gallon boiling water mixed with alum over cucumbers; let stand 24 hours. DAY 10: Drain; pour a gallon boiling water over cucumbers; let stand 24 hours. DAY 11: Drain. Combine all ingredients for pickling mixture together, bring to boil, and pour over cucumbers, covering all. DAYS 12, 13, 14: Drain each day, and reheat liquid to boiling, adding a cup sugar; pour over cucumbers. On Day 14, pack cucumbers in jars. Seal by boiling in hot water bath for 15 minutes.

"The best size for pickling is 4-6 inches in length. Don't shy away from this recipe because of the 14 days – draining and boiling take very little time, and it's fun to watch the cucumbers change into crisp, beautiful pickles!! I have used this recipe for 70 years, and now my son's family makes pickles using it. It's the best!!"

Cora Gough, Trout, Louisiana

WONDERFUL LITTLE PIZZAS

1½ cups sharp cheese, grated
1 cup ripe olives, chopped
1 (8 oz.) can tomato sauce
1 (14 oz.) can whole California
  Ortega chilies, remove veins and
  seeds and finely chop

4-5 green onions, chopped
2 garlic cloves, crushed
⅓ cup Wesson oil
1-2 loaves Pepperidge Farm
  cocktail bread, sliced

Preheat oven to 350°. Combine first 7 ingredients, mixing well. Then, spread on bread slices, and bake for 5–10 minutes, until pizza sauce is bubbly. Serve hot. Pizza spread is also good on French or sandwich bread for lunch or a light supper. The recipe makes a lot and keeps in the refrigerator a long time!

"My children love this recipe and always request it when they come home for a visit!!"

Jean Bee, New Orleans, Louisiana

LOUISIANA PLACE:
The Old United States Mint, located on Esplanade Avenue in New Orleans, was built in 1835 and is the oldest surviving mint building in this country and was the <u>only</u> mint of the Confederacy. Today, it houses exhibits on jazz and Mardi Gras.

18

CAJUN CHEESE DIP

1 lb. ground beef
2 whole tomatoes, diced
1 medium sized bell pepper, chopped
1 (16 oz.) pkg. Velveeta Mexican Cheese, cubed
2 cans Campbell's Nacho Cheese Soup Dip

Brown ground beef over medium heat, breaking up while cooking; add tomato and bell pepper. Continue to cook until vegetables wilt. Add dip and cheese to meat. Reduce heat; stir until cheeses are completely melted. Cook over low heat for 10-12 minutes more. Serve with nachos, tortilla chips, crackers, etc. A LOUISIANA TREAT!!
Serves 20–24.

Mary T. Baudoin, Thibodaux, Louisiana

CARAMEL POPCORN

2 sticks butter
1/2 cup white corn syrup
2 cups packed brown sugar
1/4 tsp. cream of tartar
1 tsp. soda
1 tsp. salt
7 qts. popped corn

In saucepan, boil first 3 ingredients for 7 minutes, stirring constantly. Remove from heat; add next 3 ingredients, stirring until mixture is foamy. Pour mixture over popped corn; mix well. Spread coated popcorn on cookie sheets or shape popcorn into balls. Place on cookie sheets. Bake at 150° for 30 minutes, turning heat off for last 10 minutes popcorn is in oven. Delicious!
Yields 7 quarts.

Nina Long, Alexandria, Louisiana

PEPPER PECANS

2 Tbsps. butter or margarine, melted   Dash of pepper
1/4 cup golden Worcestershire sauce   2 cups pecan halves
2 dashes of hot sauce

Combine first 4 ingredients; stir in pecans. Let stand 30 minutes; drain. Spread pecans evenly in a 13x9x2-inch pan; bake at 300° for 30 minutes, stirring frequently. DELICIOUS!!
Yields 2 cups.

Jean Hurley, Lafayette, Louisiana

WONDERFUL CHILI WALNUTS

3 cups walnuts, halved   1/2 tsp. ground cumin
1/4 cup oil   1/2 tsp. turmeric
2 tsps. chili powder   1 tsp. salt

Preheat oven to 325°. Place walnuts on baking sheet; roast about 20 minutes, stirring often, until walnuts are golden brown. In medium bowl, combine remaining ingredients; mix well. Then, mix in roasted walnuts, return nut mixture to baking sheet, and roast for 20 minutes more, stirring often. Drain on paper towels. Serve immediately. Easily doubled. Your family and guests will love!!
Yields 3 cups.

Jo Cart, Rayne, Louisiana

DUBLOON PUNCH

6 cups orange juice
4 jalapeno chilies, seeded and chopped

2 750-ml. bottles dry Champagne, well chilled

Combine orange juice and chilies in large bowl. Cover; refrigerate overnight. Strain orange juice into a punch bowl. Immediately before serving, add the Champagne, and gently mix. Ladle into cups.
Serves 20.

"Dubloons are silver and gold colored coins thrown from floats during Mardi Gras parades. This delicious and somewhat spicy punch is ideal for serving during Mardi Gras festivities!"

Julianne Lansing, New Orleans, Louisiana

SOUTHERN CLUB PUNCH

3 cups granulated sugar
3 qts. water
1 cup strong tea
Juice of 12 lemons
1 qt. grape or raspberry juice
Juice of 12 oranges

1 (20 oz.) can crushed pineapple
1 pt. cherries, stems removed
2 qts. ginger ale
Crushed ice
Fresh mint (optional)

Boil sugar and water together for 5 minutes; cool. Combine all ingredients, excluding ginger ale, in large container or punch bowl. Add ginger ale last and enjoy!
Yields 2 1/2 gallons!

Suzie David Stephens, Native of New Orleans, Louisiana

LOUISIANA ORANGE BLOSSOMS

2 fifths gin, chilled
1 fifth apricot brandy, chilled
48 ozs. orange juice, chilled

1 cup lemon juice, chilled
Orange bitters (optional)

First 4 ingredients should be chilled to cold. Pour all ingredients into punch bowl; mix together well. Easily halved. DELICIOUS!
Yields 36 4-ounce servings.

LUCIE LEE'S MIMOSA

8 ozs. orange juice, chilled
6 1/2 ozs. champagne , chilled

Fresh mint sprigs (optional)

Combine in pitcher, and serve in oversized, frosted wine glasses. Garnish with fresh mint. Easily doubled.
Serves 2.

Lucie Lee Lanoux, Alexandria, Louisiana

SANGRIA LOUISIANNE

1/2 cup water
1 cup sugar
2 cinnamon sticks
2 oranges, sliced

2 lemons, sliced
2 limes, sliced
1 gallon burgundy wine

Mix water, sugar, and cinnamon in saucepan. Cook to boil; cool. Strain liquid into a large crock. Add fruit; add wine; and stir 3-4 times. Let sit for 24 hours. Chill; serve cold.

Suzie Stephens, Native of New Orleans,

LOUISIANA WATERMELON DELIGHT

3 lbs. watermelon   *9 ozs. vodka*

Cut 6 small wedges of watermelon for garnish. Remove rind from remaining watermelon; seed, and cut into medium sized chunks. Put chunks and vodka in blender; blend until smooth. Strain; throw away seed remnants. Chill for an hour in freezer. Mixture should be slushy, almost frozen. Pour into tall glasses and garnish with watermelon wedges. THE ABSOLUTE BEST SUMMERTIME REFRESHER!!!
Yields 6 8-ounce servings.

SOUTHERN MINT JULIP TEA

8 cups tea   *16 ozs. bourbon*
Fresh mint, 18-20 sprigs of tender   *1 cup sugar or to taste*
  mint shoots   *Crushed ice*

Steep tea with 8 mint sprigs. Remove mint sprigs, and pour tea into large glass pitcher; add sugar; stir well. Chill tea for an hour or more. Fill iced tea glasses to the brim with ice. Gently stir bourbon into pitcher of tea: pour mixture into glasses. Place sprigs of mint about the rim of each glass. WONDERFUL VARIATION OF A DISTINCTIVELY SOUTHERN DRINK!!
Yields 8 8-ounce servings.

Carol Strickland, Native of New Orleans, Louisiana

CAFE BRULOT

Peel of 1 orange, broken up
5 sticks of cinnamon
1 Tbsp. whole cloves
6 ozs. cognac (brandy)

15 lumps of sugar
A pot of hot, strong, black coffee,
enough to fill 10 demitasse cups

Place first 5 ingredients in pan; heat. Fill a teaspoon with cognac, and ignite. Add to cognac mixture. Agitate mixture, keeping flame going. Stir with a ladle; pour coffee into flaming mixture. Fill demitasse cups, and enjoy!!
Yields 10 demitasse cupfuls.

CAFE AU LAIT

Simply combine equal amounts of hot, strong black coffee and hot milk; then, add sugar to taste. As simple as that!! Serve with beignets (page 48).

Lucie Lee Lanoux, Alexandria, Louisiana

LOUISIANA FESTIVAL:

The Jazz and Heritage Festival, in New Orleans in April, features a jazz concert aboard a steamboat, samples of the many and varied Louisiana music styles, and ethnic foods and crafts at the Fairgrounds..

SOUPS, SALADS, AND SANDWICHES

CANADIAN CHEESE SOUP

1 cup celery, chopped
1 cup bell pepper, chopped
3 cans chicken broth
3 Tbsps. butter
3 Tbsps. flour

3/4 cup cheese, grated
Salt to taste
White pepper to taste
1/2 tsp. Worcestershire sauce
Pinch of oregano

Simmer celery and pepper in broth. Strain. In heavy skillet, melt butter; stir in flour and cheese. Add cheese mixture to broth; heat. Add remaining ingredients to soup; bring to a boil. Serve piping hot. When reheating, never let soup come to a boil as it tends to separate. (If soup does separate, you can beat it back to desired consistency.)
Serves 8.

"When having guests, I have served the soup as an appetitizer in demitasse cups that I greet my guests with as they arrive!"

Liz Trammel, Dubach, Louisiana

LOUISIANA FACT:

In 1789, many French people from Canada came and settled in South Louisiana. They were called Acadians, and their descendants are often called Cajuns. The area they settled in South Louisiana is sometimes called Acadiana. The principal businesses of Acadiana are commercial fishing, fur trapping, and the farming of rice, sugar cane, and soy beans.

CRAB MEAT BISQUE WITH MUSHROOMS

CRAB MEAT BISQUE WITH MUSHROOMS

6 Tbsps. butter
4 Tbsps. onion, finely chopped
4 Tbsps. green pepper, finely chopped
1 green onion (including top), chopped
2 Tbsps. parsley, chopped
1 cup fresh mushrooms, sliced
2 Tbsps. flour

2 cups Half and Half
1 tsp. salt
1/8 tsp. pepper
1/4 tsp. ground mace
Cayenne pepper to taste
1 lb. crab meat
3 Tbsps. dry sherry

In medium skillet, heat 4 tablespoons of butter. Saute all vegetables; set aside. In large saucepan, heat remaining 2 tablespoons of butter. Remove from heat, and stir in flour; gradually, add cream. Cook, stirring constantly, until thick and smooth. Add vegetables and other seasonings. Bring to boil; reduce heat. Add crab meat; simmer, uncovered, for 5 minutes. Before serving, swish in sherry. Quick, easy, and good!
Serves 4-6.

Laura Duggan, Baton Rouge, Louisiana

LOUISIANA FACT:
The city of Baton Rouge came by its name in the late 17th century when Jean Babtiste, Sieur de Bienville first sailed up the Mississippi River. His party visited the Bayou Goula Indians on the river's west bank. de Bienville noticed a pole painted red a bit further up the river on its east bank. He called that spot Baton Rouge (red stick).

WONDERFUL SUMMERTIME MELON SOUP

2 ripe cantaloupes seeded, pared,
  and chopped
1¼ cups orange juice
1¼ cups sour cream

2 Tbsps. lemon juice
  (Fresh is best!)
4-6 orange slices

Combine first 4 ingredients; pour into a blender; mix until creamy smooth. Mixture should be chilled for an hour or more to achieve best taste! Then, pour into soup bowls, drop in an orange slice, and enjoy! A delightful southern summertime soup!
Serves 4-6.

GUMBO VERDE (GREEN GUMBO)

1 lb. Eckrich smoked sausage,
  sliced in bite sized pieces
2 cans Trappey's navy beans
1 can beef consomme with 2 cans water
1 (10 oz.) pkg. frozen chopped
  mustard greens

1 onion, chopped
1 bell pepper, chopped
Salt and pepper to taste
Garlic, chopped (optional)

Saute sausage with onions, bell pepper, and garlic. In a crock pot, combine sausage mixture with the consomme and water, beans, greens, salt and pepper. Set crock pot on low, and cook 10-12 hours. Serve in soup bowl with rice. Recipe is easily doubled. SO EASY AND SO GOOD!!
Serves 4-6 generously.

Polly Schmitz, Native of Baton Rouge, Louisiana

GUMBO YA YA

1¼ cups salad oil	1 lb. andouille sausage, sliced
2 cups flour	1 tsp. garlic, chopped
1 cup green peppers, chopped	4 bay leaves
1 cup white onions, chopped	1 tsp. dry thyme
½ cup celery, chopped	2 Tbsps. Louisiana Hot Sauce
1½ gals. chicken stock	1 Tbsp. File
1 lb. chicken, cooked and boned	½ cup green onions, chopped

In heavy saucepan, heat oil to almost smoking temperature; add flour, stirring well. Cook until roux is hazel brown, approximately 5 minutes. Add next three ingredients; cook for 5 minutes. Add stock, garlic, bay leaves, and thyme. Simmer 15-20 minutes; add chicken and sausage. Simmer 20 minutes. Add remaining ingredients. Serve with rice.
Yields 1½ gallons for approximately 12 marvelous servings!

MR. B'S BISTRO, New Orleans, Louisiana

LOUISIANA PLACE:
MR. B'S BISTRO is a truly unique restaurant. The mahogany panelled walls, hardwood floors, etched glass, and marble topped tables evoke the charm of a New York East Side bistro, while the marvelous food is a spectacular blend of contemporary Creole and New American cuisine. Owned by Ralph and Cindy Brennan who are third generation restaurateurs, Mr. B's specialities include fresh regional seafood grilled over a hickory fire, local game, signature pastas, and seasonal delights!

LOUISIANA SEAFOOD GUMBO

2 cups onions, chopped
2 cups green onions, chopped,
   tops separated and reserved
1 cup celery, chopped
1/2 cup bell pepper, chopped
6 pods garlic, chopped
2 lbs. 35 count shrimp, peeled,
   deveined, and reserving shells

1 lb. claw crab meat
1 lb. lump crab meat
1 pt. oysters, reserving liquid
1 1/2 cups oil
1 1/2 cups flour
4 qts. hot water
Salt and cayenne pepper to taste
Cooked rice

Boil shrimp shells in 1 quart unseasoned water for 15-20 minutes. Strain through cheese cloth; reserve liquid. In heavy pot, combine oil and flour to make roux. Cook over medium heat, stirring constantly until golden brown. Don't scorch! Add all vegetables and seasoning, except onion tops; saute for 5 minutes. Add strained shrimp stock; add hot water, a ladle at a time, until consistency of thick soup is achieved. Add oyster liquid, claw crab meat, and half the shrimp. Reduce to simmer; cook for approximately 45 minutes, stirring occasionally. Add remaining shrimp, oysters, lump crab meat, and green onion tops. Cook for 10-15 minutes. Season. If necessary, add water to retain volume. Serve over white rice. *Serves 10.*

Chef John D. Folse, LAFITTE'S LANDING RESTAURANT
Donaldsonville, Louisiana

ONION BRANDY SOUP

4 large yellow onions, thinly sliced
1 stick butter
2 tsps. sugar
3-4 ozs. brandy
8 cups bouillon or 5 cans bouillon
  and enough water to make 8 cups

2 Tbsps. Worcestershire sauce
Salt and pepper to taste
3 cups French bread cubes,
  buttered, sprinkled with
  Parmesan, and toasted
Swiss cheese, grated

In a saucepan that has been lined with waxed paper, cook first 3 ingredients, covered, over medium heat until onions are transparent, about 10 minutes. Remove paper, add bouillon, Worcestershire sauce, salt and pepper. Simmer for 20 minutes; then, add brandy, and simmer for 1-2 minutes more. Serve piping hot, sprinkled with toasted bread cubes, and topped with Swiss cheese. THERE'S NOTHING BETTER! A wonderful cold weather treat!!
Yields 8 delicious cupfuls!

Suzanne Reed, Ruston, Louisiana

LOUISIANA PLACE:
Fort Jesup, established in 1822 to restore order to the Neutral Strip along the border with Texas, was the westernmost outpost of the United States Army until the Mexican War. It was commanded by Zachary Taylor, who later became President of the United States. Many, the seat of Sabine Parish, was founded in 1843 as a trading post for the fort.

CREOLE VICHYSSOISE

2 Tbsps. butter, melted
2 cups leeks, cleaned and finely
  chopped
3 cups white potatoes, peeled,
  diced, cooked, and drained

2 qts. canned chicken broth
2 cups Half and Half
1 cup ham, cooked, chopped, and
  fat removed

Simmer leeks in butter only until tender; add ham, and saute 3-4 minutes. Add leeks mixture and broth to potatoes; stir, and heat. Cool; then, add mixture a cup at a time to blender; blend until liquified. Pour into large container; when soup is all blended, add Half and Half. Store in refrigerator overnight for best flavor. Heat thoroughly before serving, and garnish with fresh parsley. SUPER TASTING TREAT!!
Serves 6-8.

Carol Boudreaux, Thibodaux, Louisiana

LOUISIANA FACT:
Bayou LaFourche is the link to much that is Cajun and Southern in South Louisiana! The bayou moves leisurely for 90 miles down the length of LaFourche Parish, connecting the Mississippi River to the Gulf of Mexico. Louisianians from Thibodaux, the parish seat, to Port Fourchon call the bayou their Main Street, "The Longest 'Street' in the world." A profusion of seafood, wild game, and alligator are available to the hunter and fisherman year round!!

SO GOOD BEEF AND BROCCOLI SALAD

2 cups julienne roast beef
2 cups broccoli, chopped
4 green onions, chopped
1 jar marinated artichoke hearts
  with dressing

2 cups chicken flavored Rice-A-Roni,
  cooked per pkg.'s directions
1 cup Hellmann's mayonnaise
1 box cherry tomatoes, stemmed

Quarter artichoke hearts; reserve dressing. Combine first 3 ingredients with quartered artichokes in large bowl. Toss in rice while it's still warm. Add mayonnaise and artichoke marinade dressing; toss. Add tomatoes and seasonings to taste; gently toss. Great way to use left over roast beef!!
Serves 6.

Jean Bee, New Orleans, Lousiana

CREAMY CAJUN COLESLAW

8 Tbsps. mayonnaise
4 Tbsps. olive oil
2 Tbsps. red wine vinegar
1 tsp. Coleman's mustard
1 tsp. celery seed

1 tsp. sugar
Salt and black pepper to taste
1½ lbs. cabbage, shredded
2 carrots, shredded

Combine, and mix well first 7 ingredients; pour over cabbage and carrots. Let marinate for at least 3 hours. Easy and Good!
Serves 6-8.

John S. Walther, Thibodaux, Louisiana

HUNT'S BEST CHICKEN SALAD

6 chicken breast halves
1 bell pepper, coarsely chopped
1 onion, coarsely chopped
1 stalk celery, coarsely chopped
Salt and pepper to taste
3 stalks celery, finely chopped
4 eggs, boiled and chopped
2 Tbsps. lemon juice

3 *heaping* Tbsps. Durkee's Famous
   Sauce
1/2 cup mayonnaise (or enough to
   moisten)
1 tsp. sugar
3 Tbsps. capers
Olive slices for Garnish
Again, salt and pepper to taste

Boil chicken in water with next 4 ingredients. Remove chicken from broth; add vegetables; cool; bone. Be sure there is no gristle or skin in boned chicken chunks. Mix chicken chunks with remaining ingredients. Serve on individual lettuce leaves, and garnish with a dab of mayonnaise and olive slices. SO GOOD!
Serves 6-8.

"This recipe makes a wonderful chicken salad sandwich spread. You will have enough spread for about 24 delicious whole sandwiches!"

Adelaide Hunt, Ruston, Louisiana

LOUISIANA FESTIVAL:
Super Derby Festival in Shreveport in September, is a week of special competitions pageants, and entertainment which surround Super Derby, one of this country's richest thoroughbred races held at Louisiana Downs .

SADIE'S BEST BROCCOLI SALAD

2 bunches broccoli, diced and
  peeled, stalks and all
1 small red onion, chopped
10-12 slices bacon, fried
  crisp and crumbled

½ cup white raisins
2 tsps. vinegar
2 tsps. sugar
1 cup Hellmann's mayonnaise

Combine first 4 ingredients. Mix next 3 ingredients; pour over broccoli mixture. Chill; marinate for an hour before serving. Delectable!!
Serves 6.

Sadie Randleman, Shreveport, Louisiana

FAVORITE EIGHT LAYER SALAD

1 large head lettuce, cleaned,
  drained, and torn
1 cup celery, finely chopped
1 cup bell pepper, finely chopped
1 purple onion, sliced and separated

1 can sweet peas, drained
1 qt. Hellmann's mayonnaise
1 lb. Cheddar cheese, grated
1 lb. Mozzarella cheese, grated
Bacon bits

In a large salad bowl, layer each ingredient in the order listed. Refrigerate. Sprinkle bacon bits over all before serving.
Serves 9-12.

Iva Melancon, Sulphur, Louisiana

LOUISIANA EXPRESSION:
La vie est a moitie finie avant que l'on sache enquoi elle consiste. LIFE IS HALF SPENT BEFORE ONE KNOWS WHAT LIFE IS!! So true, so true!!!

EASY CREAMY FRUIT SALAD

2 large pkgs. Jello *instant* vanilla
  pudding
1 qt. buttermilk
1 (8 oz.) container Cool Whip

1 large can fruit cocktail, drained
2 large cans mandarin oranges,
  drained
1 cup nuts, chopped (optional)

With wire wisk, combine, and mix pudding and buttermilk. Fold in Cool
Whip. Fold in fruits, add nuts, and refrigerate. The fruit salad keeps well in
the refrigerator for several days. You may use other fruits if you like;
cherries, pineapple, and coconut are delicious too!!

Jo Tatum, Dubach, Louisiana

CALLIE'S POPPY SEED DRESSING FOR FRESH FRUIT

1/3 cup vinegar
3/4 cup sugar
1 tsp. salt
1 tsp. dry mustard
1 1/2 Tbsps. bottled onion juice

1/3 cup oil
1 tsp. poppy seeds
Assortment of your favorite fresh
  fruits

Combine first 5 ingredients in a blender. Then, very slowly, add oil and
poppy seeds to vinegar mixture, mixing well. Recipe is easily doubled.
Cut fruit into chunks, and drizzle dressing over fruit chunks. SO GOOD!

Callie Parkman, Ruston, Louisiana

LOUISIANA GREEN SALAD

7 cups packed assorted greens, bib
 and red leaf lettuce, Romaine and
 Endive, cleaned and torn
$1/2$-$3/4$ lb. bacon, crisply fried and
 crumbled
$3/4$-1 cup black olives, sliced

$3/4$-1 cup green olives, sliced
$1 1/2$ cups zucchini, sliced in strips
1 cup yellow squash, sliced in strips
$1/2$ cup purple onion, finely chopped
$1/2$-1 cup carrots, shredded
4 ozs. Parmesan cheese, grated

In large bowl, place ingredients as follows: lettuce, black olives, green olives, zucchini, yellow squash, onion, and carrots. Toss, cover, and chill for an hour. Just before serving, sprinkle with bacon and cheese. Spoon Best Salad Dressing over salad. Lightly toss.
Serves 6-8.

BEST SALAD DRESSING

1 cup Wesson oil
$3/4$ cup red wine vinegar
4 Tbsps. sugar
2 garlic cloves, finely chopped
$1/2$ tsp. salt
1 tsp. celery salt

$1/2$ tsp. Louisiana Hot Pepper Sauce
1 tsp. Worcestershire Sauce
1 tsp. fresh ground pepper
$1 1/2$ tsps. dry mustard
Dash of white pepper
$1/4$ tsp. prepared (wet) mustard

Combine all ingredients in jar with tight fitting lid; shake well. Serve over favorite greens. Delicious! Keeps refrigerated for a week.
Yields $1 3/4$ cups.

Carol Strickland, Native of New Orleans, Louisiana

DELICIOUS PASTA SALAD

1 (16 oz.) pkg. garden style twirls
   cooked per pkg.'s directions
1 (6 oz.) can sliced ripe olives
1 (2 oz.) jar pimentos, chopped

1 bunch green onions, chopped
Salt and pepper to taste
Tabasco to taste

Cool noodles. Toss together well all ingredients. Toss again in salad oil dressing (recipe below).

Lucie Lee Lanoux, Alexandria, Louisiana

MOPPIE SMITH'S SALAD OIL DRESSING

GARLIC VINEGAR:

Pod of garlic, chopped
1 pt. white vinegar
1/4 tsp. cloves

Heaping tsp. allspice
1/2 tsp. celery seed

Combine all ingredients, set aside for 2-3 days, and remove garlic. Use vinegar in following dressing.

DRESSING:

1 egg, beaten well
1 tsp. salt
1 tsp. sugar
1 tsp. prepared mustard

Dash paprika
3 Tbsps. garlic vinegar
Dash of pepper
1 3/4 cups salad oil

Combine first 7 ingredients. Add oil slowly, and beat well. Wonderful on pasta and tossed green salads.!

Yields 2 cups.

Jeanne Verlenden, GREAT FLAVORS OF LOUISIANA

GRANDMOTHER'S SALAD MOLD POT POURRI

1 (8 oz.) can crushed pineapple
1/4 cup granulated sugar
2 (3 oz.) pkgs. lime jello
8 ozs. cream cheese, softened
1 (5 oz.) can evaporated milk,
  chilled and slightly whipped

1 cup pecans, coarsely chopped
1/4 cup cherries, chopped
1 cup miniature marshmallows

Boil pineapple and sugar for 5 minutes. Pour pineapple mixture over jello; stir. Add cream cheese; mix well. Fold milk into jello mixture; add cherries, pecans, and marshmallows. Pour mixture into a 6-cup mold that has been sprayed with Pam. Chill until set. Garnish with thin slices of cream cheese and a few cherries. SO PRETTY!
Serves 6-8.

"My grandmother gave me this recipe. I remember her making this every year for special occasions until her death in 1983. Now, I am carrying on her tradition."

Beth Loeffler, Alexandria, Louisiana

LOUISIANA FACT:
The Civil War Battle of Pleasant Hill, fought in Northwest Louisiana, produced a major Confederate victory over the superior Union forces. This victory so angered Union soldiers that they went on a rampage of burning and looting of many of Louisiana's plantations as well as the burning of the city of Alexandria.

NEW ORLEANS SHRIMP REMOULADE

3 Tbsps. mustard
1/2 cup vinegar (Tarragon
    is best.)
2 Tbsps. tomato catsup
1 Tbsp. paprika
1 tsp. salt

1 clove garlic, finely chopped
1 cup salad oil
1/2 cup green onion tops, minced
1/3 cup celery, finely chopped
4 lbs. shrimp, cooked and shelled

Mix together well first 6 ingredients. Add oil, beating carefully. Add green onions and celery. Pour marinade over shrimp; marinate overnight. Serve cold on lettuce leaves and watercress. Delicious and so easy!
Serves 8.

Margaret Correro, New Orleans, Louisiana

BEST SHRIMP BOIL

4 lbs. shrimp, washed
3-4 qts. water (enough to cover all)
1 onion, quartered
2 lemons, cut up

1 pkg. crab boil
1/2 cup salt
1-2 tsps. Tabasco

In large heavy pot, combine all ingredients, except shrimp; bring to a rolling boil, and let boil for 8-10 minutes. Add shrimp; return to a boil. Remove from heat; let stand for 2 minutes. Drain, peel, and clean.

Compliments of Louisiana's Seafood Promotion and Marketing Board

BEST EVER SPINACH 'N MANDARIN ORANGE SALAD

1 bag fresh spinach, cleaned and coarsely chopped

1-2 (11 oz.) cans mandarin oranges, drained

1 box fresh mushrooms, sliced

1/2 lb. or more bacon, cooked and crumbled up

In a large salad bowl, layer all 4 salad ingredients as listed (spinach first, etc.). Cover with Debby's French Salad Dressing, toss, and serve. THERE'S NOTHING BETTER!! WONDERFUL!!
Serves 6-8.

DEBBY'S FRENCH SALAD DRESSING

2/3 cup olive oil
1/3 cup red wine vinegar
1 heaping tsp. salt
1 heaping tsp. pepper

3 heaping tsps. French's (wet) yellow mustard
4 heaping tsps. Lea and Perrin
1 clove garlic, minced

In a bowl, combine all ingredients together, mixing well. Pour into jar with top, and shake well. Pour over Best Ever Spinach 'N Mandarin Orange Salad, and enjoy!! This dressing keeps well outside of the refrigerator and is easily doubled, tripled, etc.

Debby Flowers Edgerton, West Monroe, Louisiana

LOUISIANA FESTIVAL:
The ARK-LA-MISS Fair in Monroe in September provides a showcase for Louisiana and her neighbors.

SO GOOD SWEET POTATO SALAD

2 lbs. sweet potatoes, pared and cut
   into ³/4-inch pieces
4 cups water
1/2 cup plain yogurt
1 cup Hellmann's mayonnaise
1 bunch green onions, finely chopped,
   tops and all

1/4 cup fresh parsley, chopped
1 Tbsp. fresh ginger
1/2 tsp. lime rind, grated
1 Tbsp. fresh lime juice
1/2 tsp. pepper
Salt to taste

Boil potatoes in water until tender but NOT mushy. Remove; pour into good sized mixing bowl. Separately, combine remaining ingredients. Gently stir mayonnaise mixture into cooked potatoes. Refrigerate until cold, and sprinkle with additional parsley before serving. So pretty and good!
Serves 6 generously.

OLIVE'S POTATO SALAD

6 medium red potatoes, cooked, peeled,
   and diced
2 eggs, hard boiled and diced
1/2 tsp. salt
1/2 tsp. pepper

1 shake of celery seed
1/2 cup mayonnaise
1 tsp. prepared mustard
2 tsps. sweet pickle relish
1/2 tsp. onion, grated

Combine first 5 ingredients; mix well. Separately, combine next 3 ingredients; pour over potato mixture. Grate onion over all; thoroughly mix. Let season in refrigerator for several hours before serving. Wonderful!
Serves 6-8.

Ellen Reynolds, GREAT FLAVORS OF LOUISIANA

LYDIA FITZGERALD'S TOMATO ICES

2 cups canned tomatoes
1 cup crushed pineapple
2 ozs. cream cheese
1/2 cup cottage cheese
1 cup Hellmann's mayonnaise

Salt and pepper to taste
1/2 tsp. grated onion
Pinch of ginger
1/4 tsp. Tabasco
Dash of red food coloring

Combine all ingredients, and mix in blender. Pour in paper cups or individual molds; freeze. Serve on lettuce topped with mayonnaise. SO GOOD!
Serves 6.

Lucie Lee Lanoux, Alexandria, Louisiana

MARVELOUS TOMATOES ROSE

4 large tomatoes, peeled and thinly sliced
1/4 cup celery, finely chopped
1/4 cup green onion, finely chopped
1 envelope Italian Salad Dressing Mix

3 Tbsps. vinegar
1/3 cup oil
1/2 cup Rose' wine

Place tomatoes in a shallow dish. Combine ingredients; pour over tomatoes. Cover, and chill for several hours. Serve on lettuce leaves. QUICK, EASY, LOOKS, AND TASTES GREAT!! Easily doubled.
Serves 6.

Nina Long, Alexandria, Louisiana

NEW ORLEANS PO BOY

FRIED OYSTERS: 1/4 cup flour   1/8 tsp. salt   1/2 tsp. pepper
                   1 cup vegetable oil   12 raw oysters, freshly shucked

Mix first 3 ingredients. Heat oil to hot (350°). Dip oysters in flour mixture. Fry oysters until golden, about 1 minute each side. Drain; keep warm.

TARTAR SAUCE: 1 Tbsp. lemon juice   1/2 tsp. dry mustard   1/4 tsp. salt
                  1 large egg   2/3 cup oil   1/4 cup dill pickle, chopped

Combine first 4 ingredients and a third cup oil; whip mixture on high until well blended. With blender running, gradually pour remaining oil; blend until mixture is thick. Add dill pickle; refrigerate.

SANDWICH: 2-3 large lettuce leaves   1/2 large ripe tomato, sliced
              1 Tbsp. lemon juice   Loaf of French bread

Split loaf open; cut to within 1/2 inch of other side. With halves together, put loaf on baking sheet; heat at 300° for 3 minutes. Spread sauce on bread halves. Lay lettuce and tomatoes on one half, oysters on other; sprinkle oysters with lemon juice.

Cynthia Kavanaugh, Ruston, Louisiana

LOUISIANA FACT:
A trip to Louisiana is not complete without having a Po Boy. The Oyster Po Boy is but one of a variety of Po Boys and is called the peacemaker. It is said that the Po Boy got its name because of one man's domestic distress! This (19th century) New Orleans man spent the night in the French Quarter, and the next morning was faced with the prospect of returning home to an angry wife. Thus, as an act of contrition, he took her a delicious Oyster Po Boy. From all accounts, he was forgiven!!

CREAM CHEESE AND PINEAPPLE SANDWICHES

1 (8 oz.) pkg. cream cheese, softened
1 (8 oz.) can crushed pineapple
   in heavy syrup, well drained
1/2-3/4 cup pecans, finely chopped

1/4 cup pineapple preserves
1/2 cup mayonnaise (Enough to
   make mixture spread well.)
Whole wheat or white bread

Mix all ingredients together well. Spread on bread. This spread also is wonderful used as an appetizer!!
Yields 8 deliciously different sandwiches!

CREAM CHEESE AND OLIVE SANDWICHES

1 (8 oz.) pkg. cream cheese
1 small jar green olives without
   pimento, finely chopped
1 cup pecans, finely chopped

1/2 cup mayonnaise (Enough to
   make mixture spread well.)
Whole wheat or French bread

Mix all ingredients together well. Spread on bread. This spread is also super used as an appetizer!
Yields 8 super sandwiches!

LOUISIANA FACT:
Louisiana is often called the Creole State. This is because many Creoles, people of French and Spanish descent, live in Louisiana.

GRANDMA'S SHRIMP SALAD SANDWICHES

1 cup shrimp, cooked and chopped
  (fresh or canned)
1 (3 oz.) pkg. cream cheese, softened
1/3 cup Hellman's mayonnaise
2 Tbsps. Heinz catsup
1/4 cup fresh parsley, finely
  chopped (optional)

1 1/2 tsps. prepared mustard
1/8 tsp. garlic powder
1/4 cup celery, finely chopped
1 tsp. onion, finely chopped
8 slices Pepperidge Farm white
  bread (thickly sliced)

Mix well first 9 ingredients in the order listed. Make sandwiches, and garnish with parsley, if desired. This shrimp salad is also wonderful served as a salad on lettuce leaves or as stuffing for a whole tomato! *Makes 4 super sandwiches!*

Jeanne Verlenden, GREAT FLAVORS OF LOUISIANA

LOUISIANA FESTIVAL:
Contraband Days, held during the first two weeks of May in Lake Charles, is a parish wide bonanza of good times which celebrates the legacy of Southwest Louisiana! Contraband Days takes its name from the legend that Gentleman Pirate, Jean Lafitte, sailed the area lakes and rivers hiding his "contraband" treasure along the shores of Lake Charles where it remains hidden to this day. This special festival features lighthearted historical re-enactments, sailboat regattas, Cajun Days, dances, jazzfest, band-fest, arts and crafts shows, parades, ski shows, a carnival midway, music and food!

BREADS

FRENCH BEIGNETS

½ cup boiling water	½ pkg. dry yeast
2 Tbsps. shortening	¼ cup warm water
¼ cup sugar	1 egg, beaten
Dash of salt	3 ¾ cups flour, sifted
½ cup evaporated milk	Powdered sugar

Pour boiling water over next 3 ingredients. Add milk; let stand until warm. Dissolve yeast in warm water; add milk mixture and egg. Stir in 2 cups flour; beat. Add enough flour to make soft dough; cover and chill. Roll dough to ¼ -inch thickness. Cut into squares; fry in hot oil. Brown both sides; drain; sprinkle with sugar. Serve with cafe au lait (page 24). Yields 2½ dozen.

BANANA NUT BREAD

¼ lb. butter	2 cups flour
1 cup sugar	½ tsp. salt
2 eggs	1 tsp. baking powder
4-5 ripe bananas, mashed	½ cup pecans, chopped

Cream butter with sugar. Add eggs, one at a time; blend. Beat bananas into butter mixture until smooth. Sift flour with salt and baking powder. Gradually, add flour to banana mixture; fold in pecans. Bake in buttered, floured 9x5-inch loaf pan in preheated 350° oven for 1 hour.

Jo Cart, Rayne, Louisiana

Jo Cart is not only a wonderful cook! She is also Editor and Publisher of the RAYNE FREE AND INDEPENDENT PRESS newspaper!!

NEW ORLEANS FRENCH BREAD

2 envelopes dry yeast
2 Tbsps. sugar
1 Tbsp. salt
2 1/2 cups warm water (105°F -115°F)

7 cups bread flour
Butter
To make glaze:
Beat 1 egg white with 1 tsp. water.

In large bowl, sprinkle first 3 ingredients over water; let stand until dissolved. Stir to blend; let stand until foamy, about 10 minutes. Add 5 cups flour to yeast mixture, stirring to incorporate. Stir in another cup flour. Turn dough out onto floured surface. Knead in remaining cup flour; continue kneading until dough is smooth and elastic, about 10 minutes. Butter large bowl; add dough, turning to coat entire surface with butter. Cover; let rise in warm draft free area until doubled in volume, about an hour. Punch dough down; let stand 15 minutes at room temperature. Butter 4 18-inch baguette pans. Knead dough 3-4 times; divide evenly into 4 pieces. Roll each piece into a 7x15-inch oblong. Roll up as for jelly roll; set seam side down in pan. Using a razor blade, make 3-4 3/8- inch deep cuts atop each loaf. Brush with glaze. Let stand for an hour or until dough rises to top of each pan. Preheat oven to 450°; bake loaves for 15 minutes. Reduce temperature to 350°; continue baking until bread sounds hollow when tapped on bottom, about 30 minutes. Remove from pans. Freezes well.
Makes 4 delicious loaves!

Julianne Lansing, New Orleans, Louisiana

BEST PEANUT BUTTER BREAD

3/4 cup all purpose flour
Dash of salt
1/2-1 tsp. cinnamon
1 tsp. baking powder
3 Tbsps. sugar
1/3 cup peanut butter (Your choice-
    smooth or crunchy)

1 large egg, beaten
1 tsp. Wesson oil
1 tsp. (plus a little) vanilla extract
1/2 cup sweet milk

Preheat oven to 350°. Sift first 3 ingredients together in a good sized bowl; mix well. Add next 5 ingredients; mix until well blended. Mixture will be dry. Combine vanilla and milk. Gradually add milk mixture to peanut butter mixture. Mix until well blended. Spray a 4x4-inch loaf pan with Pam. Pour in batter. Bake for 25-30 minutes or until bread is light brown. Cool in pan! EASY AND GOOD! CHILDREN LOVE!!

Billie Taylor Gough, Native of Jena, Louisiana

LOUISIANA FACT:
On April 9, 1682, the Frenchman, LaSalle, discovered the place that the Mississippi River empties into the Gulf of Mexico. LaSalle placed a cross in the river's mud and claimed all the land for France and named this land, Louisiana, in honor of France's King Louis XIV.

CAJUN SAUSAGE BREAD

1 lb. hot sausage
2-3 cloves garlic, finely chopped
3 cups Cheddar cheese, grated
1-1½ cups green onions, finely chopped, tops and all

½ cup green pepper, finely chopped
2 jalapeno chilies, finely chopped
3 Tbsps. butter, melted
2 (16 oz.) loaves frozen bread dough, thawed

In heavy skillet over medium heat, cook sausage and garlic until sausage is brown. Remove; drain on paper towels. In medium bowl, combine sausage, cheese, onions, bell peppers, and chilies. Grease 2 baking sheets. On floured surface, roll out each dough piece to a 9x13-inch rectangle. Put dough on sheets; spread half of sausage mixture evenly over each piece of dough, leaving a half inch border. Roll up as for jelly roll. Brush with butter; bake at 350° until golden brown, about 35-40 minutes. Great as a meal with a salad or served as a snack during ball game watching!

Jeanne Verlenden, GREAT FLAVORS OF LOUISIANA

LOUISIANA PLACE:
Acadian Village, Cajun Capitol of the world, is located just south of Acadiana's capital city, Lafayette. This village serves as a monument to the proud culture of the Acadian people. It offers an authentic replication of 19th century Acadian society.

SALLY ANN'S POTATO CHEESE BREAD

1½ garlic cloves, very finely
  chopped
1 tsp. butter, melted
2 cups unbleached all purpose flour
1 Tbsp. dry mustard
1 Tbsp. baking powder
½ tsp. salt

½ stick butter
1 cup sharp cheese, grated
1 cup baking potato, peeled,
  cooked, and semi-mashed
1 egg
Milk
Butter

Cook garlic in butter for 2-3 minutes, stirring constantly. In large bowl, combine next 4 ingredients, mixing well. Cut in butter; mixture will resemble coarse meal. Stir in garlic, potato, and cheese, mixing well. Make hollow in center of potato mixture. Break egg into measuring cup, beating slightly; fill cup with enough milk to make ½ cup. Stir. Pour egg mixture into hollow. Stir dough on floured surface; knead until smooth, about 15 times. Form dough into ball, place in a buttered 9-inch cake pan, and pat out to fill pan. Lightly score dough in 8-10 wedges. Dot with butter, and bake in a preheated 375° oven until golden brown, about 40 minutes. Serve warm. SO GOOD!!

Nancy McIntyre, GREAT FLAVORS OF LOUISIANA

LOUISIANA FACT:
Vacationing in Louisiana in 1990 will be the absolute best!! This is because Louisianians are planning LOUISIANA OPEN HOUSE 1990, which will be a year long celebration of all that makes Louisiana special!!

RADIO BEER BREAD

1 can (12 oz.) beer, room
  temperature
2 Tbsps. sugar

3 cups self rising flour
1/4 cup butter, melted

Mix together well first 3 ingredients; place in well buttered 9x4x3-inch bread pan, and pour butter on top. Bake at 350° for 50 minutes. Bread will be crumbly if sliced hot. You must play radio while baking bread!! Serves 6-8.

SWEET POPPY SEED BREAD

2 eggs
1 1/2 cups sugar
2 cups flour
1 tsp. salt

3 tsps. almond extract
3/4 cup cooking oil
1 cup milk
1/2 cup poppy seeds

Mix all ingredients well. Bake in 2 loaf pans or 4-5 small loaf pans which have been greased and floured. Bake at 350° for an hour.

PIRATE'S PANTRY COOKBOOK, Junior League of Lake Charles, Louisiana

LOUISIANA FESTIVAL:
The Annual Gumbeaux Gator Tail Cook Off Craft Fair, in Lake Charles in October, provides excitement for both participants and observers!!

ANNE'S DELICIOUS ROLLS

1 cup milk, scalded
5 Tbsps. butter or margarine,
  cut in small pieces
1/2 cup sugar
1 egg, beaten

1 pkg. yeast, dissolved in 2/3 cup
  lukewarm water
4 cups self rising flour
Vegetable cooking oil

In large bowl, pour milk over butter; stir until butter has melted. Add sugar; mix well. Add egg; add dissolved yeast, and mix again. Add flour, a cup at a time, mixing well after each addition. If mixture is too sticky to handle, add more flour. If using right away, turn out on floured surface. Knead lightly a few times; roll out to 1/2-inch thickness. Cut out rolls with biscuit cutter; fold over Parkerhouse style. Place on greased baking sheet, cover with kitchen towel; let rise for 1 1/2 hours. Bake at 425° for 8-10 minutes. If dough will not be used within 2 hours, lightly oil top to prevent hardening. Cover with plastic wrap, and refrigerate in a bowl. Pinch off as needed, but use within 48 hours. So good!! Everyone loves!!! *Yields 5 dozen.*

Ellen Woodruff Reynolds, GREAT FLAVORS OF LOUISIANA

LOUISIANA FESTIVAL:
Holiday in Dixie, in Shreveport in April, is a marvelous ten day celebration commemorating the signing of the Louisiana Purchase.

GLADY'S MARVELOUS CINNAMON ROLLS

1 cup milk, scalded
2 rounded Tbsps. shortening
1/4 cup sugar
1 tsp. salt
1 envelope yeast, dissolved in 1/4 cup
   warm water
1 egg, beaten
3 cups flour

4-6 Tbsps. butter
Cinnamon and brown sugar
3/4 cup nuts, chopped (optional)
For Wonderful Glaze, combine,
   mixing well:
   1 cup powdered sugar
   4 Tbsps. milk
   1 tsp. vanilla

Combine first 4 ingredients, mixing well. Cool milk mixture until lukewarm. Add yeast mixture; add egg. Add flour; mix well. Refrigerate overnight. Roll dough out to 1/4-inch thickness. Spread with butter; sprinkle with cinnamon, brown sugar, and nuts. Roll up like a jelly roll. Put in buttered baking pan; let rise about 30 minutes. Bake at 350° for 30-35 minutes. Ice with Wonderful Glaze.

Suzanne Reed, Ruston, Louisiana

LOUISIANA FACT:
The motion picture film classics, JEZEBEL with Bette Davis and Henry Fonda, A STREETCAR NAMED DESIRE with Marlon Brando and Vivien Leigh, and the recent TIGHTROPE with Clint Eastwood, are among the hundreds of films that have been made in Louisiana.

REFRIGERATOR ROLLS

1 pkg. yeast
1/4 cup warm water
1/3 cup sugar
2 tsps. salt
1 cup warm milk

1/2 cup oil
3 1/2-4 cups plain flour
1 egg
Butter

Combine first 4 ingredients. Add milk, egg, and oil. Mix; gradually, add 2 1/2-3 cups flour. Continue to add flour until dough is stiff enough to handle well. Put 1 cup flour on pastry sheet or wooden board; knead dough until smooth. Put dough in large, greased bowl; cover. Let rise until size doubles. Punch dough down; roll out to thickness of 1/2-inch. Cut rolls out with 2-inch cutter. Dot each roll in center with butter; moisten half the edge of each roll with water; fold roll in half. Place rolls in greased pan; let rise until size doubles. Bake at 400° for 12-15 minutes. This dough may be used for doughnuts. Cut with a doughnut or cookie cutter, fry in hot oil until brown, and sprinkle with powdered sugar. You may also sprinkle with cinnamon for cinnamon rolls! Dough may be refrigerated for a week.

Virginia McIntrye, Delhi, Louisiana

LOUISIANA PLACE:
The Emy-Lou Biedenharn Foundation, located in Monroe, is a must for visitors! It features Elsong, home of Joseph Biedenharn, first bottler of Coca Cola, the beautiful year-round Elsong Gardens, and the Bible Research Center that has a priceless collection of Bibles.

ANNETTE'S APRICOT CRUNCH COFFEE CAKE

TOPPING: 1/4 cup flour   1/4 cup sugar   1 Tbsp. cinnamon   2 Tbsps. butter

Combine and crumble ingredients; spread in bottom of greased Bundt pan.

CAKE: 1/2 cup butter   8 ozs. cream cheese, softened   1 1/4 cups sugar
     1 tsp. vanilla   2 eggs   2 cups flour
     1 tsp. baking   1/2 tsp. baking soda   1/4 tsp. salt
       powder   1/2 cup milk   12 ozs. apricot preserves

Beat butter, cheese, and sugar until fluffy. Beat in vanilla and eggs. Sift dry ingredients; add alternately with milk to butter mixture; beat until smooth. Pour half the batter into pan; spread preserves; be careful not to touch sides of pan. Add remaining batter. Bake at 350° for 50-60 minutes.

JANE WELCH'S PISTACHIO NUT COFFEE CAKE

1 box yellow cake mix   4 eggs
1 (3 oz.) pkg. Pistachio Nut   1 (8 oz.) carton sour cream
   Pudding Mix   1/2 cup sugar
1/2 cup cooking oil   1 Tbsp. cinnamon

Cream first 4 ingredients.; mix in sour cream. Separately, mix sugar and cinnamon. Pour half cake mixture into greased Bundt pan. Sprinkle half sugar mixture into center; swirl. Pour in remaining batter; srinkle with rest of sugar mixture. Bake at 350° for an hour.

Jeanne Verlenden, GREAT FLAVORS OF LOUISIANA

SOUR CREAM PECAN COFFEE CAKE

½ cup butter or margarine, softened
1 cup sugar
3 eggs
2 cups all purpose flour

1 tsp. baking powder
½ tsp. soda
1 cup sour cream
½ cup white raisins (optional)

Cream butter and sugar until light. Add eggs, one at a time, beating well after each addition. Sift together next 3 ingredients. To creamed mixture, add flour mixture, alternately with sour cream, beating well until smooth. Stir in raisins. Pour into a greased 13x9x2-inch greased pan; sprinkle with Pecan Topping. Bake at 350° for 40-45 minutes.

PECAN TOPPING

¾ cup packed, light brown sugar
1 tsp. cinnamon
1 Tbsp. all purpose flour

2 Tbsps. butter or margarine
1 cup pecans, chopped

Mix first 3 ingredients. Cut in butter until mixture is coarse. Stir in nuts.

"I was fortunate to have a mother who was an excellent cook! This was a special occasion treat for holidays such as Christmas morning after the gifts were opened. Delicious served warm or cold!!"

Kathleen Drott, Pineville, Louisiana

LOUISIANA FESTIVAL:
The Catahoula Lake Festival is held in Pineville in October.

ORANGE CRUNCHY ROLLS

*1 pkg. cloverleaf, brown
  and serve rolls*
4-6 Tbsps. butter, melted

2 Tbsps. orange peel, grated
1 cup granulated sugar
Orange juice

Tear apart cloverleaf rolls(in 3 sections). Place on cookie sheet; brush with butter. Mix peel and sugar with enough orange juice to moisten. Turn each roll in mixture until well coated. Bake per rolls' package's directions. These rolls are super for brunch, morning coffees, really anytime!!

Liz Trammel, Dubach, Louisiana

SUSAN'S BEST MONKEY BREAD

1 stick butter (No substitutes!)
1 cup milk
*1 pkg. yeast, dissolved in 1/4 cup
  warm water*
1/4 cup sugar

2 eggs, beaten
1/2 tsp. salt
3 cups flour
1 stick butter, melted

Scald 1 stick butter and milk; cool. Add remaining ingredients to milk mixture, <u>except</u> 1 1/2 cups of flour. Beat with wooden spoon; add rest of flour. Cover mixture with damp cloth; refrigerate overnight. When ready to bake, pour butter into a Bundt pan; drop dough by spoonfuls into pan. Bake at 375° for 40 minutes. Pull apart to serve. Very Impressive Bread to be So Easy!

Susan Atwood, Great Flavors of Louisiana

WHIPPING CREAM BISCUITS

1½ cups self-rising flour   *½ pt. whipping cream*   *Butter*

Mix flour and cream until blended. Butter hands well; form dough into ping-pong sized balls. Place on baking sheet an inch apart. Bake at 425° for 10-12 minutes or until golden brown. Easily doubled. Freezes well; place dough balls on cookie sheet in freezer. When frozen, remove balls from sheet; store, frozen, in plastic bags. Delicious and Easy!!
Makes 2½ dozen large or 3½ dozen small biscuits.

RIVER ROADS COOKBOOK II, Junior League of Baton Rouge, Louisiana

The Junior League of Baton Rouge has sold over 300,000 copies of its marvelous cookbook, RIVER ROADS II.

QUICK BUTTERMILK BISCUITS

2 cups self rising flour, sifted   4 Tbsps. mayonnaise   1 cup buttermilk

Combine all ingredients, mixing into dough. Then, add a little more flour so dough will roll out easily. Roll out until dough is about ½-inch thick. Cut with biscuit cutter. Bake at 400° until biscuits are golden brown.
Yields 12 delicious biscuits!

Linda White, Natchitoches, Louisiana

LOUISIANA FESTIVAL:
The Natchitoches Christmas Festival takes place each year in December. The entire downtown area lights up in a gorgeous display of Christmas color with a fireworks display that has attracted as many as 150,000 people! The Lights of Natchitoches continue each night through New Year's.

LORA LEE'S CHEESE 'N CHIVE MUFFINS

4 cups all purpose flour
2 tsps. baking powder
1 tsp. salt
1 tsp. baking soda
¼ cup butter, cut into pieces

6 ozs. sharp Cheddar cheese,
  grated
¼ cup fresh chives, finely chopped
2 cups buttermilk
1 egg, beaten

Preheat oven to 350°. Sift together first 4 ingredients. Cut in butter until mixture looks like coarse meal. Stir in cheese and chives. Combine buttermilk and egg; add to dry ingredients; stir until blended well. Batter will be thick. Bake at 375° in greased muffin tins for 30 minutes. Serve hot with real butter. Great with country suppers and wonderful for breakfast!
Yields 24 delicious muffins!!

NICE 'N EASY APRICOT MUFFINS

1¾ cups flour
3 Tbsps. sugar
2 Tbsps. brown sugar
2 Tbsps. honey
4 Tbsps. shortening
4 tsps. baking powder

1 cup milk
2 eggs
⅔ cup pecans, chopped
½ cup dried apricots, chopped
Pinch of salt
15 large paper muffin cups.

In a large bowl, mix well first 11 ingredients. Fill muffin cups until two-thirds full. Bake at 375° for 25 minutes. Incredibly Good!!
Yields 15 marvelous muffins!!

Joyceline Breckenridge, Thibodaux, Louisiana

BLACK IRON SKILLET CORN BREAD

1 cup yellow corn meal	*1 tsp. sugar*
1 cup flour	*1 egg, slightly beaten*
4 tsps. baking powder	*1 cup milk*
¾ tsp. salt	*2 Tbsps. shortening, melted*

Sift together first 5 ingredients; add egg and milk; mix well. In skillet, combine shortening with corn meal. Bake at 425° for 25 minutes.

Compliments of Louisiana's Office of Tourism

SOUTHERN CORN PONE STICKS

1⅔ cups yellow corn meal	*⅔ cup boiling water*
1½ tsps. salt	*2 Tbsps. butter, softened*
¼ tsp. baking soda	*½ cup buttermilk*

Combine first 3 ingredients. Add butter; stir in boiling water; stir until butter melts. Stir in buttermilk; pour mixture into greased corn stick pan. Bake at 425° for 20 minutes. Great with fresh garden vegetables.
Yields 8 very crispy and crunchy corn pone sticks!

Barbara H. McMillan, Franklinton, Louisiana

LOUISIANA PLACE AND FESTIVAL:
The Mill Branch Settlement, in Franklinton, features authentic log cabins assembled in village format which illustrates pioneer life. The Settlement is home to the Washington Parish Free Fair, held each year in October.

VEGETABLES
and
SIDE DISHES

BEST TOP STOVE APPLES

1½ cups sugar
1 cup water
1 tsp. lemon juice

8 apples, peeled and cored
Several drops red or green food
coloring, if desired

In skillet, combine sugar and water; boil. Add lemon juice and food coloring. Put apples in skillet; cook over low heat; turn apples at least once. Apples are done when "fork tender." Cooked apples may be stuffed with chopped pecans and raisins. Delicious alone or with the stuffing!!

Mrs. Harry G. Frazer, Sr., Monroe, Louisiana

LOUISIANA SPICED CANTALOUPE

7 lbs. cantaloupe, peeled and cut
into 1-inch pieces (8-10 large
cantaloupes)

3 lbs. sugar
8 cinnamon sticks
1 Tbsp. whole cloves

In a large, heavy pot, combine all ingredients; cook for about 1½ hours or until fruit has become transparent. Pour into sterile jars; seal. Serve with wild game, fowl, or meats. Delicious and Southern!!
Yields about 10 pints.

LOUISIANA PLACE:
The Creole Nature Trail, in Southeast Louisiana near Lake Charles, features over a hundred species of wildlife including the alligator. The trail begins in Sulphur and winds south through the great marshlands, beaches, and wildlife refuges of Cameron Parish.

VICTORIA'S CHEESE STUFFED ARTICHOKES

1 cup almonds, chopped and toasted   *1 cup Parmesan cheese*
3 cups bread crumbs, sifted   *4 Tbsps. olive oil*
1 dozen artichokes

Combine almonds, crumbs, and cheese; moisten with olive oil. Remove artichokes outside bottom leaves; cut about $1/2$ inch from each top. Place artichokes in dutch oven; parboil (partially cook) for about 15 minutes. Remove from heat, coat leaves (and between) with cheese filling. Cover each artichoke with tablespoon of olive oil. Pour cup of water into dutch oven; cook artichokes over low heat for 40 minutes or until tender. Easily halved.
Serves 12 deliciously!!

Victoria Howze, Independence, Louisiana

LOUISIANA FACT:
The Battle of New Orleans, which took place on January 8, 1815, was the most one sided victory in American military history! The attacking British suffered 2,000 casualties in a little over two hours. The Americans, led by Andrew Jackson, lost seven killed and six wounded. It was a stirring victory for a very young American nation and was the last battle ever fought between Britain and the United States!

ASPARAGUS CASSEROLE

2 cups asparagus, drained and cut   3-4 hard boiled eggs, sliced
1 cup salted almonds, chopped   1/2 cup bread crumbs

In a greased 2-quart casserole, sprinkle bread crumbs. Then, layer asparagus, eggs, and almonds. Repeat layering once. Sprinkle with additional bread crumbs. Dot with butter. Pour white sauce over all. Bake 15-20 minutes or until hot in a 400° oven.
Serves 6-8.

JOANNA'S THICK WHITE SAUCE

6 Tbsps. butter, melted   2 cups evaporated milk, diluted
1/2 tsp. salt   1 (4 oz.) can mushrooms, chopped
6 Tbsps. flour   1/4 lb. sharp cheese, grated

Melt butter; add flour and salt, stirring constantly. Remove from burner, and stir in milk. Return to burner; stir constantly until sauce is thick and smooth. Add cheese and mushrooms to white sauce; stir in well. Pour over casserole. This white sauce is good with other dishes such as Macaroni and cheese. For the basic white sauce, just omit the mushrooms and cheese.

Joanna Steed, Ruston, Louisiana

LOUISIANA FACT:
In 1860, there were 1600 plantations in Louisiana. These plantations covered over 40% of Louisiana's arable land!

DICK'S MARVELOUS HOLLANDAISE FOR STEAMED VEGETABLES

3 egg yolks
1 stick butter, cut into several pieces
1 Tbsp. lemon juice or to taste

Cayenne pepper to taste
White pepper to taste

In top of double boiler, combine yolks and butter, adding butter a few pieces at a time and whisking after each addition. Add lemon juice and both peppers. Continue whisking until sauce thickens. Pour over favorite steamed vegetables, asparagus and broccoli, green beans and cauliflower. Easily doubled!
Yields 1 cup.

Ellen Reynolds, GREAT FLAVORS OF LOUISIANA

LOUISIANA'S BEST BAKED BEANS

1 lb. bacon, chopped
2 medium sized onions, chopped
1 gal. pork and beans

1/2 cup catsup
1/2 cup barbecue sauce
2 lbs. (32 oz.) bag brown sugar

Saute onions and bacon. Do not cook until brown. Pour beans into large pot; add bacon and onions. Add remaining ingredients, mixing well. Bake at 250° until thick. Wonderful!
Feeds an Army!

Linda White, Natchitoches, Louisiana

LOUISIANA FACT:
Natchitoches, Louisiana's first town, was founded in 1714 by Louis Juchereau de St. Denis as a trading post and fort.

LOUISIANA MAQUE CHOUX DELIGHT

24 ears of fresh sweet corn, cleaned
    and shucked
1 cup butter
2 medium onions, finely chopped
2 large bell peppers, finely chopped

6 large ripe tomatoes, peeled,
    seeded, and roughly chopped
2 tsps. salt
2 tsps. ground black pepper

Hold each ear of corn over large bowl, and cut away kernels in layers. (You DO NOT want to end up with whole kernels.) Scrape knife down cob, drawing all corn "milk" out. Heat butter in large pot over medium high heat; add onions, peppers, and tomatoes: saute until onions are clear, about 15 minutes. Stir in salt and pepper; add corn kernels and "milk"; stir well. Reduce heat to medium; cook until corn is tender, about 20-30 minutes. If mixture begins to dry out, add a little milk and butter.
Serves 6-8 generously.

"I like to serve Maque Choux (French for Mock Shoe) with a chicken dish on Sundays. My family loves it! Maque Choux is an old recipe made famous in Louisiana by French speaking people!"

Peggy Frankland, Sulphur, Louisiana

LOUISIANA FESTIVAL:
The Mamou Cajun Music Festival, in June, features the Queen Contest. To enter this marvelous competition, contestants must be 65 or older, able to tell a joke in French, recite Cajun recipes, and able to dance both a Cajun waltz and two-step!!

TOO GOOD CORN CASSEROLE

1 (15 oz.) can cream styled corn
2 (15 oz.) cans corn or mexicorn, drained
3 eggs, beaten
1/2 cup Cheddar or Swiss cheese, grated

1/4 scant cup corn meal
1/4 cup parsley, chopped
1/2-1 cup green onions, chopped
1/2 stick butter, melted
Dash of cayenne pepper
Parmesan cheese

Mix mexicorn with creamed corn. Add remaining ingredients; blend. Pour into buttered 9x12-inch casserole; sprinkle with Parmesan cheese. Preheat oven to 325°; bake until firm, about 40-45 minutes. Marvelous! Serves 8-10.

Anne Timmons, Brusly, Louisiana

Anne's home is Cinclare Plantation which is the northernmost active sugar plantation in the world!!

LOUISIANA PLACE:
The Cabildo, in New Orleans, is a large, three story stuccoed structure built between 1795 and 1799 by the Spanish to house their governing council. The French called it their Maison de Ville and until 1911 it housed public offices.Then, it became the Louisiana State Museum and houses exhibitions on settlement of Louisiana during the French, Spanish, and early American periods. Also housed in the museum is the Mississippi River Gallery which chronicles the place of the river in Louisiana's history.

EMMYE BOWE'S CORN BREAD DRESSING

2 cups corn meal
1 Tbsp. sugar
1 Tbsp. baking powder
1 tsp. salt
2 eggs, beaten
1 (12 oz.) can evaporated milk
¼ cup vegetable oil
2 cups fresh mushrooms, chopped
1 cup celery, chopped
1 bunch green onions, finely chopped,
  tops and all

3 Tbsps. butter, melted
3 eggs, beaten
2 (14½ oz.) cans chicken broth
1 (10 ¾ oz.) can cream of chicken
  soup, undiluted
¾ cup almonds, sliced
1 tsp. poultry seasoning
1 tsp. pepper
Dash of parsley flakes
Fresh parsley for garnish

Combine first 4 ingredients; add next 3 ingredients, mixing well. Place greased 10-inch iron skillet in preheated 350° oven until hot. Remove from oven; spoon in batter. Bake corn bread at 350° for 35-40 minutes or until lightly browned; cool. Crumble corn bread into large bowl. Saute mushrooms, celery, and onions in butter until tender. Combine corn bread, sauteed vegetables, and next 7 ingredients, mixing well. Spoon into greased 13x9x2-inch baking dish. Bake at 350° for 45 minutes. Great Holiday Dish!! Serves 12.

You may make a day ahead, cover, and refrigerate. Allow dressing to stand at room temperature for 30 minutes. Bake at 350° for an hour. Enjoy!!

GREAT FLAVORS OF LOUISIANA

YOUR CHOICE FRIED FRUIT FRITTERS

6-8 apples, peaches, apricots, _or_
    pears, cut into pieces
1 cup flour
1 tsp. sugar

1/2 tsp. salt
2/3 cup milk
2 eggs, well beaten
Powdered sugar

Set fruit aside. Mix together well next 3 ingredients; slowly add milk. Next, add eggs; blend. Dip fruit in batter; fry in deep hot fat (375°) for 3-5 minutes or until golden brown. Drain on paper towels. Sprinkle fruit with powdered sugar, and serve with Scrumptious Lemon Sauce. So Southern!!

SCRUMPTIOUS LEMON SAUCE

1/2 cup sugar
3 tsps. cornstarch
1 cup boiling water

Juice of 1/2 lemon
Rind of 1/2 lemon, grated
1 Tbsp. butter

In saucepan, mix sugar and cornstarch; stir in boiling water. Add remaining ingredients. Boil, stirring constantly, until mixture is transparent. Serve over fritters or on puddings (Carrot pudding, page 134)!

Carol Colclough Strickland, New Orleans, Louisiana

LOUISIANA FACT:
The first movie house in the United States was Vitascope Hall, which opened in New Orleans in 1896.

71

CREOLE GREEN BEANS

1 onion, chopped
2 stalks celery, chopped
1 bell pepper, chopped
3 (15 oz.) cans cut green beans, drained

6 slices bacon, fried and drained
1 (15 oz.) can stewed tomatoes
1 tsp. sugar
Salt and pepper to taste

Saute first 3 ingredients in 2 tablespoons bacon grease until vegetables are limp. Add tomatoes; simmer for 10 minutes, adding sugar. Add beans; season; simmer 5 minutes more. Pour into casserole; crumble bacon over top. Heat at 350° for 20 minutes. Easy, and good!!
Serves 8.

Cynthia Kavanaugh, Ruston, Louisiana

GREEN BEAN BUNDLES

2 (17 oz.) cans whole, uncut green
   beans, drained
1/2 lb. bacon
1/2 cup brown sugar

1 1/2 Tbsps. cornstarch
1/4 cup vinegar
3 Tbsps. soy sauce
1 (6 oz.) can pineapple juice

Make 8-10 serving sized bundles of beans. Wrap each bundle with bacon slice; secure with toothpick. Place bundles in flat pyrex baking dish. Broil until bacon is crisp and brown. In top of double boiler, make sauce by mixing together remaining ingredients, making sure that cornstarch is completely dissolved. Cook sauce until thick. Pour sauce over beans; serve.
Serves 8-10.

Barbara H. McMillan, Franklinton, Louisiana

SOUTHERN FRIED PEACHES

6 peaches, pared and split   *12 tsps. brown sugar*
2 Tbsps. butter, melted

In iron skillet, drop peaches, pitted side up, into butter. Fill each peach hollow with teaspoon of sugar; let peaches simmer until well cooked and tender. Serve as a dessert with ice cream or topped with whipped cream or as a condiment with meats. The fried peaches are particularly good with roast lamb or grilled lamb chops! Delicious!

SUSANNA'S BEST BAKED POTATOES

4 large baking potatoes, washed   *1 cup green onions, chopped, tops*
*   and baked 1 hour at 450°*   *   and all*
8 bacon slices, crisply fried,   *Salt and pepper to taste*
*   drained, and chopped*   *1 cup (or more) Cheddar or*
1½-2 jalapeno chili peppers,   *   Mozzarella cheese, grated*
*   seeded and finely chopped*   *1 (8 oz.) carton sour cream*

Cut, and scoop out potato pulp. Combine next 3 ingredients. Add pulp, seasonings, half the cheese, and sour cream; combine by gently stirring. Fill potato hulls with potato mixture. Sprinkle remaining cheese on top. Broil until cheese melts, watching carefully. WONDERFUL!!
Serves 8 generously!

OLD SOUTHERN SECRETS COOKBOOK, GEMS OF ANTE-BELLUM DAYS

CREOLE POTATOES

16 small new potatoes, each
   quartered
1½ tsps. Creole Seasoning

¼ cup butter or margarine, melted
½ cup parsley, chopped
Parsley sprigs for garnish

Place potatoes in steamer rack over boiling water. Cover; steam 12-15 minutes or until tender. Transfer potatoes to a bowl; sprinkle with seasoning. Add butter and parsley. Toss, coating potatoes thoroughly. *Serves 8.*

Jean Hurley, Lafayette, Louisiana

CREOLE SEASONING

¼ cup salt
1 Tbsp. powdered garlic
1 Tbsp. pepper, freshly ground
1 Tbsp. paprika

¾ tsp. powdered onion
¼ tsp. cayenne pepper
½ tsp. dried thyme, crumbled
¼ tsp. dried oregano, crumbled

Mix together all ingredients. Store in glass jar. As easy as that! So good on roasted or grilled meat, poultry, and seafood. Also adds zest to potato and corn dishes! Easily doubled.
Yields about ¾ cup.

MR. B'S BISTRO, New Orleans, Louisiana

LOUISIANA FESTIVAL:
The National Day of the Acadians is celebrated in Lafayette in August.

HE-MAN POTATOES

1/2 lb. Velveeta cheese
1 pt. Half and Half
4 1/2 ozs. Cheddar cheese, shredded
1 stick margarine

Dash of salt and pepper
1 (2 lb.) pkg. frozen hash
   brown potatoes
2 onions, sliced (optional)

Melt first 4 ingredients over medium heat. Add salt and pepper. Place potatoes on top of onions in 9x13-inch dish. Pour cheese mixture over potatoes; bake, uncovered, at 350° for an hour. Good with brisket (page 87). Serves 8.

Laurie Kent, Lake Charles, Louisiana

CAJUN ONION RINGS

White onions, (1 per person),
   refrigerated overnight, peeled
Flour
Salt

Cayenne and black pepper
Garlic powder
Cooking oil

Mix 4 dry ingredients in paper bag. Add onion slices, a few at a time; shake until well coated. In heavy pot, fry in hot oil until onions are brown and float to top. Remove; drain on paper towels. Serve immediately.

"Let two Cajuns cut up an onion, and you have a treat!!"

J.J. "Joe" Champeaux, Jack Kemmerly, Lake Charles, Louisiana

PIRATE'S PANTRY COOKBOOK, Junior League of Lake Charles

CAJUN DRESSING

1 lb. hot bulk pork sausage
1 lb. mild bulk pork sausage
1 large onion, chopped
1 large bell pepper, chopped
3 stalks celery, chopped

2 (.375 oz.) envelopes instant
  chicken noodle soup mix
2 cups regular rice, uncooked
6 cups water

Brown together both sausages, stirring to crumble; drain. Stir in remaining ingredients; then, pour into a 3-quart casserole, cover, and bake at 350° for an hour. Uncover, and cook for 15-20 minutes more.

MARVELOUS RICE AND CHEESE CASSEROLE

3 Tbsps. butter, melted
1 yellow onion, chopped
1 garlic clove, minced
1/4 cup fresh parsley, chopped
1 1/2 cups chicken broth

1 cup uncooked rice
3/4 cup dry white wine
3/4 cup Parmesan cheese, grated
Parsley for garnish

Saute onion and garlic in butter for 8 minutes; parsley for last 4 minutes . Stir in next 3 ingredients; bring to boil. Cover; cook over low heat until liquid is absorbed. Mix in cheese, garnish, and serve. Super side dish!!

LOUISIANA FACT:
Louisiana is a top rice producing state, and rice is an important ingredient found in a preponderance of Louisiana cuisine. Louisiana cooking is distinctive, in part, because of the varied creative use of rice in a multitude of delicious dishes.

LOUISIANA SPINACH 'N DUMPLINGS

3 (10 oz.) bags fresh spinach, cleaned   1/4 tsp. salt + 1/4 tsp. white pepper
4 Tbsps. butter   1 cup sharp Cheddar cheese, grated
4 Tbsps. flour   1/8 tsp. Tabasco or to taste
3/4 cup Half and Half   1/2 cup bread crumbs, browned

Cook spinach in boiling water, covered, for 3 minutes. Rinse with cold water; drain, saving juice. Squeeze out all spinach juice; chop finely. Make sauce by melting flour and butter; add remaining ingredients, cook over medium heat until thick, stirring constantly. Combine sauce and spinach. By teaspoonfuls, spoon dumplings into spinach mixture. Gently stir, folding in dumplings. Cover with bread crumbs. Serve hot. So Delicious and Different!!

DUMPLINGS

1 cup milk   1/2 tsp. salt
2 eggs, beaten   Fresh nutmeg, grated
6 1/2 Tbsps. flour

Combine flour and milk to smooth consistency. Pour into eggs; add salt and nutmeg. Cook in top of double boiler until firm, about an hour. Do not stir! Then, combine with spinach according to recipe above.

Julianne Lansing, New Orleans, Louisiana

LOUISIANA EXPRESSION:
Une bonne conscience fait un bon oreiller! A CLEAR CONSCIENCE IS A GOOD PILLOW!

QUICK 'N EASY SQUASH CASSEROLE

1 bag frozen squash
1/2 tsp. salt
1/2 tsp. white pepper
2 Tbsps. margarine

1 egg
1/2 cup onions, chopped
Crumbs of 6 Ritz crackers
1 cup Cheddar cheese, grated

Cook squash; mash. Add next 6 ingredients mix well. Pour into a 1 quart casserole, sprinkle the cheese on top, and bake at 350° for 25 minutes. *Serves 4-6.*

Ethel DeLoge, Baton Rouge, Louisiana

DELICIOUS CORN STUFFED SQUASH

8 small squash
2 cups corn (Fresh is best!)
1 cup squash pulp
1 cup dry bread crumbs
1 tsp. salt

3 strips bacon, fried crisp and
  chopped, reserving drippings
1/4 tsp. pepper
Butter

Boil squash until tender; scoop out each center. Fry corn in bacon drippings; add squash pulp and remaining ingredients. Fill shell with squash mixture, sprinkle with additional bread crumbs, and dot with butter. Bake at 400° for 15 minutes. Wonderful!!
Serves 8.

"For a variation, you may prepare eggplant exactly the same way!!"

Victoria Howze, Independence, Louisiana

LOUISIANA FESTIVAL:
The Italian Festival, in Independence in April, celebrates the rich heritage of the Italians who made Louisiana their home.

STRAWBERRY PRESERVES

6 cups fresh strawberries, washed
    and stems removed
4 ¾ cups sugar

4 Tbsps. lemon juice (Fresh is
    best.)
5-6 (8-oz.) glass jars with tops

Combine strawberries and sugar; let sit for 4-5 hours. Bring berries to simmer over low heat; add lemon juice. Raise heat, and bring berries to rapid boil; boil for 10-12 minutes until berries are clear, and syrup is thick. Remove from burner, and skim the top. Cover; let stand until cold. Pour into jars, seal, and put sealed jars into large pot. Cover jars with water, boil for 15 minutes. After water bath, preserves will keep for a year!

FIG CONSERVE

2 lbs. ripe figs, washed and
    cut in pieces
1 cup crushed pineapple
2 medium lemons, cut in
    small pieces

½ tsp. salt
1 cup pecans, chopped
4½-5½ cups sugar or an amount
    equal to figs mixed with
    pineapple and lemons

Mix figs with pineapple and lemons; put into top of double boiler with equal amount of sugar. Add salt. Bring slowly to boiling point; simmer gently until thickened, but still a bit runny. Stir in nuts. Delicious!!
Yields about 3 pints.

RIVER ROAD COOKBOOK I, Junior League of Baton Rouge

LOUISIANA FACT:
The Junior League of Baton Rouge has sold over _one_ _million_ *copies of RIVER ROAD I, a must for every cookbook collection!!*

STEED'S BEST SWEET POTATO CASSEROLE

3 cups sweet potatoes, mashed	*1 tsp. vanilla*
1 cup sugar	*1 stick margarine, softened*
2 eggs, well beaten	*1 (7 oz.) can coconut*

Mix all ingredients together well, and pour into a large casserole. Cover with Best Holiday Topping. Bake at 300° for 75 minutes. Easily doubled or halved, can be frozen and thawed before cooking, and can be prepared a day ahead and refrigerated. SO GOOD AND SO EASY!!
Serves 8.

BEST HOLIDAY TOPPING

1 stick margarine	*1/2 cup self rising flour*
1 cup brown sugar	*1 cup pecans, chopped*

Mix all ingredients together well. Spread over sweet potato mixture.

"Once you make this as a holiday dish for your family, you will be asked to make it year after year and not just for holiday meals!"

Kathy Myers Steed, Shreveport, Louisiana

LOUISIANA FESTIVAL:
Christmas in Roseland, in Shreveport, begins each year the day after Thanksgiving and continues through New Year's Eve.

SCALLOPED TOMATOES AND ARTICHOKE HEARTS

1 (12 oz.) can whole tomatoes
1 (14 oz.) can artichoke hearts
1/2 cup onions, finely chopped
2 Tbsps. shallots, chopped

1/4 lb. butter
1/2 tsp. basil leaf
2 Tbsps. sugar
Butter to grease casserole

Preheat oven to 325°, and butter a shallow casserole. Drain tomatoes and artichokes. Rinse artichokes twice; then, quarter. Saute onions and shallots in 2 tablespoons butter, until they are tender. Add tomatoes, artichokes, and all remaining ingredients to onion mixture; heat in pan for 2-3 minutes, stirring gently. Pour mixture into casserole, and bake at 325° for 10-15 minutes. A DELICIOUS LOUISIANA DISH!!

Polly Schmitz, Native of Baton Rouge, Louisiana

LOUISIANA FESTIVAL:
The River City Blues Festival, in Baton Rouge in April, provides one and all with the satisfying sounds of harp and horn sounding out all manner of human joys along with human trials and tribulations!

SYLVIA'S LAST OF THE CROP GREEN TOMATO PICKLES

8 cups whole small green tomatoes or
4 large green tomatoes, halved
1½ qts. iced water
⅔ cup salt
2 cups bell peppers, thinly sliced
1 large can pimento (for color)
2 cups onions, sliced

SYRUP:
2 cups sugar
2 cups vinegar
2 Tbsps. mustard seed
2 Tbsps. celery seed

Peel tomatoes. Make brine by combining water and salt; soak tomatoes in brine for an hour. Pour off brine. Make the syrup by combining sugar, vinegar, and mustard and celery seeds. Boil syrup mixture for 5 to 10 minutes before adding tomatoes. Cook tomatoes in syrup for 10 minutes; then, add other vegetables, and cook for 5 minutes more. Fill sterilized jars, and cover with the syrup. Remove any air bubbles, wipe sealing edge, and seal with new lids. Process in boiling water bath canner for 5 minutes. Remove immediately from the water, and let stand to develop flavor.
Yields 4 pints.

"These pickles taste particularly good at a Louisiana fish fry which will always feature Louisiana Farm Raised Catfish!!"

Sylvia Buckley, Trout, Louisiana

LOUISIANA FACTS:
Oil, often called "Black Gold" was discovered in Louisiana in 1901. Natural gas was discovered in 1916.

MEATS AND MAIN DISHES

CAJUN ROUND STEAK FINGERS

1 large round steak, trimmed of
   all fat and cut into small strips
3/4 cup all purpose flour
2 tsps. salt
1 Tbsp. dehydrated onion

1 tsp. garlic powder
Enough black pepper to make
   mixture almost black
Enough red pepper for mixture to
   show some red

Set steak aside. In a bowl and using your hands, combine and mix well the remaining ingredients. Continue mixing until mixture is gooey, using a small amount of water if necessary. Mixture MUST get gooey and sticky. Add steak; mix again, thoroughly covering steak strips. Cover tightly with plastic wrap; refrigerate for 6-8 hours. Before cooking, roll each steak strip in dry flour. Then, in hot vegetable oil, fry strips to desired "doneness."
Serves 3-4.

"My daughter-in-law introduced this to our family 10 years ago. (The first meal she prepared for us.) Her recipe reads add black pepper until mixture is black, and red pepper until mixture is red. This is a little too Cajun for small children but delicious! These steak fingers are unusually tender. Venison steaks are also delicious prepared this way!"

Kathleen Drott, Pineville, Louisiana

LOUISIANA EXPRESSION:
Laissez le bon temps rouler! LET THE GOOD TIMES ROLL!!

MARY'S GRILLADES AND GRITS

4 lbs. chuck _or_ round steak, cut in bite sized pieces
1 cup flour
2 cups onion, chopped
3 cloves garlic, finely chopped
2 cups bell pepper, chopped
1/2 cup celery, chopped
4 (10 oz.) cans beef broth
1 (16 oz.) can whole tomatoes, liquid included, all liquified in blender
2 Tbsps. sugar
1/2 tsp. thyme
Salt, black and red pepper to taste
1 1/2 cups vinegar
1/2 cup green onions (optional)
Hot grits

Combine vinegar, salt, and peppers; cover steak; marinate overnight. Drain meat, roll in flour; brown in heavy skillet. Remove. In same skillet, saute next 4 ingredients until tender. Add next 4 ingredients and meat; simmer until meat is tender, approximately 2 hours. Serve over grits topped with green onions. Superb!!
Serves 12.

From the Kitchen of Mintmere Plantation House, New Iberia, Louisiana

LOUISIANA PLACE:
Mintmere Plantation House, built in 1857, was originally the main house for a 480 acre sugar cane plantation. During the Civil War, Mintmere was known as the "sweetheart's parting point" because many young men leaving for service in the Confederate Army would board ships anchored at the plantation's steamboat dock. Today, Mintmere, the oldest house native to Iberia Parish, is a bed and breakfast inn and open daily for tours!

LOUISIANA BEST STEAK MARINADE

1/3 cup fresh lemon juice
2 Tbsps. dry mustard
1/4 tsp. salt
1 Tbsp. coarsely ground pepper
1/2 cup Worcestershire sauce

1/2 tsp. Accent
1 clove garlic, crushed
1/2 cup soy sauce
1 1/2 cups salad oil
Steaks of your choice!

Combine all ingredients, mixing well. Put in container that has top. Shake well. Pour over steaks; marinate for 3-4 hours. Grill or broil steaks. This marinade is the best! It also tenderizes as it marinates.

Barbara McMillan, Franklinton, Louisiana

ITALIAN CASSEROLE

1 can crescent rolls
1 lb. ground beef or sausage
2 (10 oz.) cans Rotel
1 onion, chopped

Italian seasoning to taste
1 (6 oz.) can mushrooms, drained
2 pkgs. Mozzarella cheese slices

Brown meat; add next 4 ingredients, simmering until onions are tender. In a greased 1 1/2-quart casserole, lay crescent rolls out flat on bottom. Add meat mixture; lay cheese slices on top. Cook at 375° for 30 minutes or until top is brown. A wonderful "busy day" supper.
Serves 4-6.

Carol Jo Fuller, Dubach, Louisiana

LOUISIANA FESTIVAL:
The Louisiana Cattle Festival is held in Abbeville in October.

LUCILLE'S HAS-IT-ALL CREOLE CASSEROLE

2 medium eggplants, boiled until
   tender and chopped
1 medium onion, minced
1/2 bell pepper, minced
1 1/2 cups Italian bread crumbs
2 cups Cheddar cheese, grated

2 Tbsps. butter
1 lb. ground beef
1 can crab meat or 1/2 lb. sausage
2 eggs, beaten
1/2 cup black olives, sliced
Salt and pepper to taste

Saute onion and pepper in butter until tender. Brown meat. (If using sausage, crumble, mix with beef, and brown together.) Mix all ingredients together well; pour into buttered 2 1/2-quart casserole. Sprinkle more bread crumbs on top. Bake at 400° for 30 minutes. A delectable complete meal in itself! Easily doubled or halved.
Serves 8-10.

OVEN BAKED BEEF BRISKET

5-6 lbs. beef brisket (Have your
   butcher trim off excess fat.)
1 cup wine (Any type does nicely!)

1/2 pkg. dry onion soup mix
1 Tbsp. Worcestershire Sauce

Place brisket on heavy duty foil. Put in pan that has tight fitting lid. Make marinade by combining wine, soup mix, and Worcestershire. Pour over brisket. Wrap tightly, cover pan, and let marinate overnight. Bake at 250° for 5-6 hours, basting 2-3 times. Easy and delicious!
Serves 10-12.

Lucille T. Robison, Lecompte, Louisiana

REAL FAST-REAL HOT CAJUN CHILI

1 lb. lean ground beef
1 lb. hot sausage, sliced into 1/2-inch
   pieces
6 slices bacon, cut into 1/2-inch pieces
1 cup onion, chopped
1/2 cup bell pepper, chopped
2 cloves garlic, chopped
1 jalapeno pepper, chopped
1/4 cup Lea and Perrins

3/4 cup red wine
1 tsp. dry mustard
1 tsp. celery seeds
2 Tbsps. chili pepper
2 (16 oz.) cans tomatoes
3 (15 oz.) cans red kidney beans
Tabasco to taste
Salt and pepper to taste

In heavy pot brown first 3 ingredients; drain. Add remaining ingredients, cover, and simmer for about 1 1/2 hours until thickened. Adjust seasonings, and let stand 10 minutes before serving. You may use microwave – Cook first 3 ingredients on high for 7-8 minutes: drain. Add remaining ingredients, cover, and cook on high for 15 minutes, stirring 3 times. Continue cooking at 50% power for 30 minutes or until thickened. Either way, this chili is DELICIOUS!!

Yields 5 quarts.

"Good for a crowd on a cold night!!"

Mary Kurzweg, Metairie. Louisiana

LOUISIANA FACT:
The longest bridge in the world is found in Louisiana. It is the 29 mile Lake Pontchartrain Causeway which crosses Lake Pontchartrain and provides the most direct route from New Orleans to points north.

CREOLE GOULASH

2 (15 oz.) cans red kidney beans
1/2 lb. sliced bacon, crisply cooked,
   reserving drippings
1 (16 oz.) can tomatoes

1 tsp. baking powder
1/4 lb. Cheddar cheese, grated
Salt and pepper to taste

In heavy skillet, add beans to bacon drippings. Combine tomatoes with baking powder; add to bean mixture. Stir all together well. Season with salt and pepper; let mixture simmer for 2-3 minutes. Pour mixture into 2-quart casserole, cover, and bake at 325° for an hour. Sprinkle with cheese, arrange bacon strips over all, and bake, uncovered, for 10 minutes more. *Serves 6 generously.*

Carol Colclough Strickland, Native of New Orleans, Louisiana

BREAKFAST PIZZA

1 lb. sausage, browned
   and crumbled
1 can crescent dinner rolls
1 cup cheese, grated

4-5 eggs
1/2 cup milk
Salt and pepper to taste

Press out rolls in a pizza pan (or big, round pan). Sprinkle sausage on top of rolls. Combine remaining ingredients together; pour on top of sausage. Bake at 375° for 15 minutes. So easy, and your family will love!! *Serves 6.*

Glenda Fuller, Dubach, Louisiana

SOUTH LOUISIANA RED BEANS AND RICE

1 lb. dried red beans, rinsed
2 qts. water
1 big ham bone
1½ lbs. Italian sausage
2 cloves garlic, chopped
2 onions, chopped

2 stalks celery, chopped
2 bay leaves
Salt and pepper to taste
6 green onions, finely chopped,
  tops and all
Cooked rice

In big pot, place beans and ham bone in water. Saute sausage with garlic. When sausage is browned, drain, and add to beans. Add next 5 ingredients. Bring mixture to boil. Simmer for 2-3 hours. If needed, add additional water. When done, remove ⅛ cup beans; mash. Add back to cooked beans. Serve over mounds of rice. Great with corn bread (page 62)!
Serves 8-10.

LOUISIANA DIRTY RICE

1 cup ground chicken livers
  and gizzards
1 Tbsp. parsley, chopped
1 cup ground beef

½ cup onion, chopped
2 Tbsps. butter
2 cups rice, cooked
Salt and pepper

Saute first 4 ingredients in butter until onion is brown. Mix with rice, season with salt and pepper, and serve hot.
Serves 4 generously.

Suzie Stephens, Native of New Orleans, Louisiana

LOUISIANA FESTIVAL:
The International Rice Festival is held in Crowley in October.

CAJUN MEAT LOAF

1/2 stick butter, melted
1 cup yellow onion, chopped
1/2 cup green pepper, chopped
2-3 cloves garlic, finely chopped
1 tsp. cayenne pepper
1/2 tsp. thyme
1 tsp. freshly ground pepper
1/2 tsp. cumin

1 1/4 lbs. ground chuck or round
1 egg, beaten
3/4 cup quick cooking oats
3/4 cup catsup
1-2 tsps. Lea & Perrins
3/4 cup sharp Cheddar cheese,
  grated (optional)

Preheat oven to 375°. In skillet with butter, add next 7 ingredients; cook until vegetables are tender, stirring often. In a bowl, combine meat, egg, oats, half cup catsup, Lea & Perrins, and cheese. Blend in vegetables. Form into loaf in a 9 1/2x5x3-inch loaf pan. Bake for 20 minutes; spread top with quarter cup catsup; bake for 40-45 minutes more. Wonderful and easy!!

Jeanne Verlenden, GREAT FLAVORS OF LOUISIANA

LOUISIANA PLACE:
Louisiana Hayride, nicknamed "Cradle of the Stars" and located in Bossier City, helped launch the careers of 23 country music and rock-n-roll stars including Elvis Presley, Hank Williams, Johnny Horton, and Johnny Cash! A museum there pays tribute to these stars.

DELICIOUS MEXICAN ZUCCHINI DISH

*1 pkg. Martha White's Mexican
  Cornbread Mix*
6-8 good sized zucchini, chopped
6 Tbsps. margarine
1 large onion, chopped
1 large bell pepper, chopped

*1 can Rotel tomatoes and green
  chilies*
2 eggs, well beaten
1½ cups Cheddar cheese, grated
Bread crumbs (optional)

Make cornbread mix according to package's directions; bake, and crumble. In margarine, saute zucchini, onion, and bell pepper until tender. Combine cornbread and vegetables with tomatoes and eggs; mix well. Pour mixture into 9x13-inch pyrex dish. Top with cheese and bread crumbs. Cook at 350° until cheese melts, and casserole bubbles. You may substitute (4 medium) eggplant or yellow squash for zucchini. A super side dish or delightful "meatless meal!"
Serves 6-8.

Jo Tatum, Dubach, Louisiana

LOUISIANA NOTABLE:
Jimmy Davis is a two term governor of Louisiana who was one of eleven children of tenant farmers. He sang on street corners to pay for his education and wrote YOU ARE MY SUNSHINE which is the Official Song of Louisiana. The former governor has a master's degree and an honorary Doctorate in Music from Louisiana State University.

SOUTH LOUISIANA OKRA CASSEROLE

1 lb. Jimmy Dean Sausage
1 cup onions, chopped
1/2 cup celery, chopped
1/2 cup bell pepper, chopped
1 clove garlic, chopped
1 chicken bouillon cube

1 (8 oz.) jar Old El Paso Taco
  Sauce (hot or mild)
1 tsp. sugar
1 lb. fresh or frozen okra, sliced
1 cup Uncle Ben's Rice, cooked per
  pkg.'s directions

In skillet, fry sausage until all pink disappears, and most of liquid evaporates. Remove sausage; drain on paper towels. Saute onion, celery, pepper, and garlic in drippings until onions are transparent. Move vegetables to side of pan; blot up excess liquid. Return sausage to skillet; add next 4 ingredients; saute over medium high heat until okra is cooked. Stir in rice, cover, and simmer for 10-15 minutes. If necessary, add 1/2 cup of water, and adjust seasonings. DELICIOUS!!

Estelle Trahan Tortorich, Native of Plaquemine, Louisiana

LOUISIANA FESTIVALS:
The International Acadian Festival and Parade, in Plaquemine in October, features an exciting bayou ceremony which heralds the arrival of Evangeline, heroine of the poem by Longfellow. This poem was written, in part, by Longfellow while he was in Louisiana!

The Okra Festival is held in Kenner in June.

DESPERATION MEAL

4-6 medium pork chops
1 large onion, chopped
1 can (14½ oz.) whole tomatoes
½ bell pepper, chopped
1 rib celery, chopped

½ cup green onion tops, chopped
½ cup parsley, chopped
Salt and pepper to taste
2 (6 oz.) pkgs. wild rice

Brown chops and onion in large skillet. Add next 6 ingredients. Cook for 20 minutes over low heat. Add wild rice to chops using ½ amount of water called for on packages. Stir well; cook, covered, for 30 minutes until liquid is gone. Quick, easy, and wonderful!!
Serves 4-6.

"You may substitute chicken for the pork chops, but the skin should be removed. This is a marvelous "busy day," one dish meal!"

Dinah Bradford, Lake Charles, Louisiana
PIRATE'S PANTRY COOKBOOK, Junior League of Lake Charles

LOUISIANA FACT:
Lake Charles, renowned for its warm Cajun hospitality and wonderful Creole cuisine, is appropriately called "The Treasure City" of Louisiana's Gulf Coast! This name also stems from the marvelous legends that have grown up from the days when the swashbuckling pirate, Jean LaFitte, spent time in Lake Charles and its environs!!

AVOCADO CHICKEN

4 chicken breasts, skinned
   and boned
Salt and pepper to taste
8 Tbsps. green onions, chopped,
   tops and all

6 Tbsps. butter
1 large ripe avocado, peeled, $1/2$
   sliced and $1/2$ mashed
3 Tbsps. sherry
$3/4$ cup cream

Season chicken with salt and pepper. In large skillet, saute onions in 3 tablespoons butter for 3-5 minutes. Add chicken, and saute, covered, over low heat until chicken is tender, about 10-12 minutes. Remove chicken when cooked; set aside, keeping chicken warm. Pour sherry into skillet; bring to low boil, stirring constantly. Add remaining butter,seasoning, and cream. Gently stir in mashed avocado. Pour sauce over chicken breasts, and top with avocado slices. Serve with wild rice, green salad, and Radio Beer Bread (page 53). DELICIOUS AND UNIQUE!!
Serves 4.

Ellen Woodruff Reynolds, GREAT FLAVORS OF LOUISIANA

LOUISIANA FESTIVAL:
Louisiana has the best celebration just before Lent in the world! It's called Mardi Gras!! Many Louisiana towns and cities celebrate with Mardi Gras Parades that always take place 47 days before Easter. These communities include Covington, Grand Marais, Houma, Lafayette, Lake Charles, Loreauville, Monroe, Morgan City, New Orleans, and Slidell!

CHICKEN JAMBALAYA

2½-3 lbs. fryer, cut up
Salt and pepper
2 Tbsps. bacon drippings
½ cup onion, finely chopped
½ cup green pepper, finely chopped
½ cup celery, finely chopped
2 cloves garlic, finely chopped
Bay leaf

1 lb. can tomatoes
1 cup water
1½ cups long grain rice, uncooked
½ cup ham, cooked and diced
2 shallots, finely chopped
¼ cup parsley, minced
Several dashes Tabasco
Pinch of thyme

Season chicken with salt and pepper. In heavy pot, brown chicken in drippings until golden; remove. Brown lightly next 3 ingredients. Add next 4 ingredients and chicken; continue cooking until sauce is very hot. Add rice, and reduce heat to low; cook for an hour. When rice is almost done, add remaining ingredients; cook until done. OUTSTANDING!!
Serves 4-6.

THE OFFICIAL LOUISIANA SEAFOOD AND WILD GAME COOKBOOK

LOUISIANA FACT:
Belief has it that the Spanish brought Chicken Jambalaya to Louisiana. The Spanish called it Paella and made it only with chicken. Louisiana Creoles renamed it Jambalaya and make it with anything! Jambalaya is a well seasoned mixture of any number of combinations of meat, poultry, sausage, seafood, and vegetables which are simmered with uncooked rice until the liquid is absorbed. Jambalaya is a marvelous way of cooking leftovers and enables the cook to combine all kinds of flavors!!

MAMMY LOTT'S SUNDAY CHICKEN AND DUMPLINGS

1 hen (Do not substitute fryer!)
5 chicken bouillon cubes
2 Tbsps. salt or to taste

Black pepper to taste
2 eggs
2 cups flour, more if needed

Defrost hen; remove giblets. Place hen in large pot, and cover with water; add bouillon, salt, and pepper. Stew, covered, until tender. Remove hen from pot; cool; bone. Dip 3 cups broth from pot; cool. Broth remaining in pot should equal about 2 quarts. To 3 cups broth, add eggs. To make dough, gradually add flour to broth-egg mixture, stirring after each addition. Mix in flour until dough has consistency of biscuit dough. When dough is stiff enough to roll out, roll with rolling pin, and begin to cut out dumplings. Heat remaining broth to simmering; drop dumpling dough strips into broth. Using bowl dumplings were mixed in, add 2 tablespoons flour and small amount of water. Combine to make a "thickening." Gradually, add this to cooking dumplings. Turn burner heat to medium high; cook, covered, for 20 minutes. If necessary, stir to prevent sticking. Add chicken. Enjoy!!
Serves 8-10 generously.

"This recipe was a favorite of my mother-in-law. So, in keeping with Southern tradition, I make this when my brood gets together because it's one they all love!!"

Sylvia Buckley, Trout, Louisiana

NEWLYWED CHICKEN

1 cup onion, chopped	Dash of Tabasco
1 cup celery, chopped	Dash of garlic powder
1/2 green pepper, chopped	Dash of Tony's Creole Salt
1 Tbsp. flour	1 chicken, cut into serving sized
2 Tbsps. Wesson Oil	pieces
1 cup chicken broth	Cooked rice
Dash of Lea and Perrins	

Brown first 4 ingredients in oil. Set aside in a bowl. Brown chicken in same skillet, adding a little more oil. Add vegetables back to skillet, stir in broth and next 4 ingredients. Let simmer for 45-55 minutes to an hour, stirring occasionally. Don't let chicken stick! Serve with or over rice. *Serves 6-8.*

"This is a dish that my husband watched his mother prepare for their family of eight. He insisted that I start my collection of recipes with this one! It was the first and only dish that I could cook when we were first married!!"

Susan M. Lauve, Alexandria, Louisiana

LOUISIANA NOTABLE:
Lillian Hellman, one of the most important American playwrights, was born in New Orleans. Hallmarking Hellman's works are sharply drawn characters, outspoken themes, a taut plot, and firm, lifelike dialogue. Her works include THE CHILDREN'S HOUR, THE LITTLE FOXES, WATCH ON THE RHINE, and TOYS IN THE ATTIC. Miss Hellman won the 1941 Drama Critic's Circle Award for WATCH ON THE RHINE.

PIPKIN'S DELICIOUS CHICKEN 'N MUSTARD SAUCE

1 cup prepared mustard
1 cup comb-free honey
1/2 tsp. horseradish

6 medium sized chicken breasts,
thoroughly washed

Mix first 3 ingredients well; heat over low burner until smooth, stirring often. Place chicken on grill, away from direct heat. Brush chicken with sauce on both sides. Cook for 2 hours, brushing with sauce once every 30 minutes. Chicken may also be cooked in a 300° oven for 2 hours, basting often with sauce.
Serves 4-6.

Bob Gough, Native of Trout, Louisiana

YERGER ANDRE'S CHICKEN

1 cup raw brown (long grain) rice
1 can cream of mushroom soup,
mixed with 1/2 can water
1 (14 oz.) can artichoke hearts and
juice, each heart quartered
1 (4 oz.) can button mushrooms
4 chicken breasts

1/4 tsp. cayenne pepper
1 Tbsp. dried minced onion
2 tsps. ground black pepper or
to taste
1 1/2 tsps. Creole Seasoning (page 74)
Salt to taste
Mrs. Dash to taste

Grease 9x13-inch casserole; pour in rice and soup. Place artichokes and mushrooms evenly in casserole. Place chicken in casserole, breast side up. Top with seasonings. Bake for 45 minutes at 350° or until chicken is tender.

Martha Yerger Andre, Native of Tallulah. Louisiana

PRETTY CHICKEN CREOLE

4-5 lbs. chicken, cut up
Flour for coating chicken
Salad oil
3 medium onions, sliced
1 garlic clove, minced
1 bell pepper, chopped

1 #3 can tomatoes
1 cup beer
1 Tbsp. salt
4 cups rice, cooked
Paprika for garnish

Dust chicken with flour; brown in oil. Remove from skillet. In same skillet, saute next 3 ingredients until soft. Return chicken to skillet; add tomatoes, salt and beer. Cover; simmer over low heat for an hour or until chicken is tender. Serve topped with paprika over rice.
Serves 6-8 generously.

CHICKEN AND SAUSAGE

1 fryer, cut up
Garlic salt to taste
4 slices bacon, cut into pieces and
    fried, reserving drippings
2 medium onions, chopped
2 cloves garlic, pressed

2 tomatoes, diced
1 cup rice, uncooked
1 lb. pepperoni sausage, sliced
1/2 head cabbage, torn in leaves
2 1/2 cups water

Rub chicken with garlic salt. In bacon grease, brown chicken, adding a little oil if necessary; set chicken aside. To same skillet, add next 5 ingredients; saute until onions are soft. Simmer rice mixture for 15 minutes. Put chicken in large pot; cover with cabbage leaves. Pour rice mixture over chicken and cabbage. Add water. Cook, covered, over low burner for an hour or until liquid is gone. Top with cooked bacon.

BEST EVER CHICKEN BROCCOLI CASSEROLE

4 whole chicken breasts, boiled, boned, skin removed, and cut up, reserving broth
2 bunches fresh broccoli, cleaned, speared, steamed, and drained
1 pkg. dry Pepperidge Farm Seasoned Herb Dressing Mix
1 can cream of chicken soup
1 can cream of mushroom soup
2 cups Cheddar cheese, grated
1 (6 oz.) can sliced mushrooms, drained
Butter or margarine
Cooked rice

Lightly grease with butter a 9x13-inch glass casserole dish. Mix soups with required water; heat. In casserole dish, make several layers of chicken, broccoli, mushrooms, dressing mix, soup, and cheese. Be sure you top with cheese. Bake at 350° until bubbly, 20-30 minutes. Let casserole "set" for a few minutes before serving. Serve with rice and fruit salad (page 36). Wonderful when entertaining as well as for the family!
Serves 10.

Cheri Crouch, Alexandria, Louisiana

LOUISIANA PLACE AND FESTIVAL:
Kent House, located in Alexandria, is the oldest known standing structure in central Louisiana. The house was built by the French soldier, Pierre Baillio II, and completed in 1800. Open hearth cooking and quilting are demonstrated at Kent House from October through April. Herb Day is held in the spring, and Tradition Day, a spring festival with heritage crafts, fine arts, food, and old fashioned fun, is held every year the first Saturday in May.

SO GOOD TURKEY POULETTE

10 slices bread, toasted
1 lb. bacon or 10 slices ham,
  cooked

10 slices turkey
Parmesan cheese
Paprika

Place slices of crisp bacon or ham on toast. Cover with turkey slices; sprinkle with cheese. Cover with White Sauce, sprinkle additional cheese and paprika over sauce, and bake at 350° until sauce bubbles. Wonderful !!
Serves 8-10.

WHITE SAUCE

2 sticks butter, melted
3/4 cup flour
1 qt. milk
Salt and pepper to taste
Tabasco

2-3 Tbsps. cooking wine
2 egg yolks, beaten
1 medium onion, sliced in half
1 (6 oz.) can mushrooms, stems
  and pieces

Combine butter and flour. Gradually, add milk. Add next 4 ingredients. Add onion; cook until thick. Remove onion; add mushrooms.

"This is my very own recipe! I loved the Turkey Poulette served in New Orleans at the Roosevelt Hotel, and this is as close as I could come to that recipe!! My children love it, and it's a great way to use leftover turkey!"

Callie Ratcliff, St. Joseph, Louisiana

LOUISIANA FACT:
New Orleans' natives say that New Orleans has two seasons - summer and February! That's because New Orleans doesn't have a predictable winter of continual chill. Rather, it has a little cool with long, warm stretches in between!!

DELICIOUS CROCK POT DOVES

10 doves, 1-2 per serving
Salt, pepper, and paprika
1 cup flour
1/4 cup oil
2 cans cream of chicken soup
2 cans cream of celery soup
2 cans chicken broth

1/4 cup white wine
2 onions, chopped
1 Tbsp. green onions, chopped
1 Tbsp. parsley, minced
Rice or noodles, cooked per
    pkg.'s directions, omitting salt

Season doves with salt, pepper, and paprika; coat with flour. In skillet, heat oil; brown doves. Place doves in crock pot with next 7 ingredients. Cook on high for 4 hours. Serve over rice.

LOUISIANA'S BEST DOVES

12 doves
6 Tbsps. butter
3 Tbsps. flour
2 cups chicken broth
1/4 cup sherry

Salt and pepper to taste
2 (4 oz.) cans button mushrooms
1/4 cup parsley, minced
Wild rice, cooked

Season doves with salt and pepper. In skillet, melt butter; brown doves. Remove doves to baking dish. In same skillet, add flour to butter; stir. Add broth and sherry; season with salt and pepper; blend. Pour over doves. Add mushrooms and parsley. Bake, covered, at 350° for an hour. Serve over rice.

THE OFFICIAL LOUISIANA SEAFOOD AND WILD GAME COOKBOOK

GLAZED WILD DUCKS

6 ducks, washed and cleaned
Salt and cayenne pepper
Apples, oranges, onions, and
  celery, sliced
1 stick butter, melted

2 cups vermouth
1 (6 oz.) can orange juice
3 ozs. brandy
3 tsps. Lea & Perrins
Plenty of cooked, wild rice

Salt and pepper ducks well, inside and out. Stuff cavities with slices of apples, oranges, onions, and celery. Brown ducks in butter. Place ducks, breast side up, in baking pan. Add vermouth and a little water. Cover; bake at 275° for 2½-3 hours. Remove ducks from pan; save liquid. Let ducks cool; then, remove bones, and place meat in casserole. Add orange juice, reserved liquid, brandy, and Lea & Perrins. Cover with orange slices. Bake at 200° for 40-50 minutes. Serve over rice. A Delicious Way to Enjoy Duck!!
Serves 10-12.

Louisiana's Department of Wildlife and Fisheries, Baton Rouge, Louisiana

LOUISIANA FACT AND FESTIVAL:
Louisiana's great wildlife marshes near Cameron boast the largest duck and goose wintering population in North America. In the spring, the marshes provide some of the most exciting bird watching in North America.

The Gueydan Duck Festival is held each year in September.

VENISON WIENER SCHNITZEL

1 cup flour
1 egg, beaten
1/4 cup water
2 cups bread crumbs
1/2 tsp. salt
1/2 tsp. pepper
1 tsp. onion powder
1/2 tsp. garlic powder

1/2 tsp. dry Italian seasoning
1/2 tsp. dry mustard
1/2 tsp. celery seed
3 cups oil
2 lbs. venison cutlets, tenderized
   by pounding flat
Salt
1/2 stick butter, melted

Combine egg, water, and all dry spices; mix well. Put flour in pie pan, bread crumbs in another, and egg-water mix in a third. Heat oil in Dutch oven. Dredge meat in flour, shaking off excess. Dip in egg-water mixture; coat both sides, allowing excess liquid to drain off. Coat both sides with bread crumbs; pat slightly, and shake off excess. Fry in hot oil until golden brown, drain, and salt lightly. Drizzle melted butter over top. Serve immediately.

Serves 6-8.

"Onions may be prepared using any leftover batter and using the same procedure as for meat preparation. Corn on the cob, green vegetables, and garlic bread are tasty with this dish!"

Betty Yerger, Lake Providence, Louisiana

LOUISIANA FESTIVAL:
The Louisiana Fur and Wildlife Festival is held in Cameron in January.

VENISON SAUCE PIQUANTE

4 lbs. venison, washed, cut in
   cubes, and seasoned with salt
   and pepper
Bacon drippings
8 medium onions, coarsely
   chopped
2 bunches green onions, sliced
   diagonally, tops and all
1 bell pepper, chopped
1 cup celery, chopped
1 (6 oz.) can tomato paste

2 (8 oz.) cans Rotel tomato sauce
1 cup olive oil
2 cloves garlic, chopped
2 Tbsps. Worcestershire Sauce
Juice of 2 lemons
1 cup flour
Salt and pepper to taste
10 cups water
1 can mushroom soup
Cooked rice

In heavy skillet, fry venison in drippings; remove. In same skillet, make roux with olive oil and flour. Add tomato sauce and paste. Add both onions, bell pepper, celery, Worcestershire, lemon juice, and soup. Simmer for an hour. Add venison to soup mixture; simmer for 30 minutes. Add water, garlic, salt and pepper; cook 4 hours. Serve hot over rice. The best! *Serves 14-16.*

    Louisiana Department of Wildlife and Fisheries, Baton Rouge, Louisiana

LOUISIANA FACT:
Sauce Piquante, a sauce that is a Louisiana original, is a thick, keenly flavored sauce made with a roux and tomatoes, highly seasoned with herbs and peppers, and simmered for hours. Chicken, beef, and seafood also lend themselves to Sauce Piquante dishes! Thank goodness for Louisiana Cooks!

CRAWFISH D'LAUVE

20 lbs. live crawfish, 5 lbs. per person   *Tony's Creole Seasoning*
1 box salt   *60 qt. pot with basket*
1 (8 oz.) jar cayenne pepper   *Styrofoam ice chest*

Put 2 inches water in bottom of pot; stir in salt and pepper. Bring water to a boil. Put live crawfish in pot. Cover. When steam starts to pour from lid, reduce heat to medium; continue cooking for 4-5 minutes. Remove crawfish from pot; pour into ice chest, sprinkling seasoning generously between layers of crawfish. Cover; let stand for 5-10 minutes. Serve hot.

Lewis Lauve, Jr., Alexandria, Louisiana

ESTELLE'S CRAWFISH CASSEROLE

1 stick butter (No substitutes!)   *¼ cup parsley, minced*
2 cups onions, chopped   *1 can cream of shrimp soup*
2 cups celery, chopped   *1 can cream of mushroom soup*
2-3 cloves garlic, crushed   *½ tsp. liquid crab boil*
1 lb. crawfish tails, shelled   *1 cup Uncle Ben's Rice, cooked per*
1 (8 oz.) can sliced mushrooms   *pkg's. directions*

Saute onions and celery in butter until soft but not brown; add garlic. When garlic becomes aromatic, stir in tails and continue stirring over high heat for 5-6 minutes. Add next 5 ingredients; simmer to blend for 10-15 minutes. In 2½-quart casserole, combine crawfish mixture with rice. Bake at 350° for 15-25 minutes until bubbly.

Estelle Trahan Tortorich, Native of Plaquemine, Louisiana

CRAWFISH AND SAUSAGE JAMBALAYA

1 lb. smoked sausage, thinly sliced
1 cup vegetable oil
1 medium onion, chopped
1 cup green onions, chopped
1 cup celery, chopped
1 cup parsley, chopped
1 (8 oz.) can tomato sauce

1 tsp. thyme
1 bay leaf
1 Tbsp. Creole Seasoning (page 74)
1 tsp. cayenne pepper
2 cups raw long grain rice
1 (13 oz.) can chicken broth
1 lb. crawfish tails

In heavy frying pan, fry sausage over medium heat; drain on paper towels. In heavy pot, saute next 4 ingredients in oil until wilted. Add tomato sauce; stir into vegetable mixture several minutes. Add rice, broth, and all seasonings; simmer over medium low heat for 10 minutes, stirring occasionally. When rice has absorbed almost all water, add crawfish. Continue cooking until rice is cooked. TRULY A LOUISIANA DISH!! *Serves 6-8.*

Lucille Landry, Thibodaux, Louisiana

LOUISIANA FACT AND FESTIVAL:
Louisiana is first in the nation in the production of crawfish and shrimp and leads the nation in overall seafood production!

Louisiana's annual Jambalaya Festival is held in Gonzales in June.

THE GOVERNOR'S CRAWFISH ETOUFFEE

1 lb. crawfish tails and fat	1 can cream of mushroom <u>or</u>
1 large onion, chopped	cream of celery soup
1 medium bell pepper, chopped	Salt and pepper to taste
3 stalks celery, chopped	Red pepper to taste
1 stick butter	Cooked rice

Saute onion, bell pepper, and celery in butter. Add salt and pepper, and allow seasonings to wilt. Add tails and fat to seasonings, and cook over low heat until tails curl up and turn pink. Finally, add soup and about a third of a cup of a water. Cook for about 30 minutes over medium heat; then, serve over rice. DELICIOUS!!
Serves 4.

Governor Edwin W. Edwards
Currently Serving as Louisiana's Eighty-Third Governor

LOUISIANA FACT AND FESTIVAL:

Louisiana's state capitol building, completed in 1932, is the tallest state capitol building in our country. It is 34 stories high. Engraved on the 49 steps that lead to its entrance are the names of all 50 states. Alaska and Hawaii are both engraved on the top step!

The Breaux Bridge Crawfish Festival, held in April, features crawfish races and marvelous fais-do-dos (street dances).

BAYOU SHRIMP CASSEROLE

2 cups rice, cooked
2 (10 oz.) pkgs. frozen broccoli
  cooked per pkg.'s directions
1 lb. Velveeta cheese, melted
1 can cream of shrimp soup
1 lb. shrimp, boiled and peeled
1 cup onions, finely chopped
1 clove garlic, finely chopped
3 Tbsps. butter
Ritz cracker crumbs

Add soup to cheese, heat; be careful not to burn cheese. Saute onions and garlic in butter; add to cheese mixture. Add rice and broccoli to mixture; gently stir. Add shrimp. Top with crumbs; heat at 300° until bubbly. *Serves 6-8.*

Marsha Spell, Shreveport, Louisiana

CREVETTES AU HERBSAINT

2 lbs. shrimp, peeled and cleaned
4 Tbsps. butter
2 Tbsps. Herbsaint (or any other Anise
  flavored liqueur)
2 Tbsps. shallots, finely chopped
3/4 cup heavy cream
Salt and fresh pepper to taste
2-3 cups rice, cooked

Stir fry shrimp in butter until pink, 3-4 minutes. Add Herbsaint; stir. Remove shrimp; add cream and shallots to skillet; and cook over high heat, stirring constantly for a minute. Add salt and pepper; return shrimp to sauce, heating through, stirring constantly. Serve over rice.

"This is such __fun__ to cook!! Our guests join us to prepare it. We first had this dish in New Orleans and loved it so much that we came home and have done our very best to recreate it! It is wonderful and serves 4 generously!"

Mary Kurzweg, Metairie, Louisiana

FATHER'S FAVORITE SHRIMP ETOUFFEE

1 stick butter per lb. of shrimp (which
   have been peeled and cleaned)
1 large onion, chopped
3 stalks celery, sliced
1 medium bell pepper, chopped
1 clove garlic, minced

Salt and pepper to taste
Cayenne pepper to taste
1 Tbsp. tomato paste (for color)
1 cup water mixed with 1 Tbsp.
   cornstarch
Cooked rice

In melted butter, saute next 4 ingredients until limp. Stir in tomato paste, and add shrimp; simmer, stirring for 1-2 minutes. Stir in water and cornstarch mixture; simmer, stirring often, for about 8 minutes or until shrimp are pink, and mixture is thickened. Season to taste, and serve over hot rice.

"This shrimp etouffee was a great favorite of my father's, and my mother was truly a master in its production!!"

Cynthia Kavanaugh, Ruston, Louisiana

LOUISIANA FACT AND FESTIVAL:

Etouffee is a method of cooking that is very popular in Louisiana. It is a manner of cooking, usually with shrimp or crawfish which has been smothered in chopped vegetables, over a low flame until all are tender and Louisiana Good!!

The Louisiana Shrimp and Petroleum Festival and Fair is held annually in Morgan City in September.

LOUISIANA MUSTARD SHRIMP 'N CORN BREAD

*1/2 cup green onions, cut diagonally
into 1/2-inch slices*
4-5 Tbsps. Wesson Oil
24-30 raw jumbo shrimp, shelled
2-3 shallots, minced
1/2 cup dry white wine

1/2 cup heavy cream
1 stick butter, cut into small pieces
2 1/2 Tbsps. ground mustard
Salt and white pepper to taste
*Lemon juice, freshly squeezed and
to taste*

Heat oil over high heat; stir fry shrimp for 2-3 minutes or until pink. Lower heat to medium; saute shallots for 1 minute. Add wine, scrape up any browned bits; stir in cream. Cook for 4 minutes, until mixture thickens. Lower heat, stir in butter and mustard. Do not let boil!. Add salt, pepper, lemon juice, and shrimp. Separately, saute onions. Serve over corn bread, 4-5 shrimp per serving; top with onions.

CORN BREAD

1 cup buttermilk
1 tsp. baking soda
1 cup flour
1 cup yellow corn meal

3/4 tsp. salt
2 large eggs
2 Tbsps. butter, melted
Butter for greasing pan

Preheat oven to 450°. Butter well an 11x17-inch jelly roll pan. Combine milk and soda; set aside. In blender, mix next 3 ingredients. With blender on, pour in milk, eggs, and butter; blend well. Pour mixture into pan; smooth top. Bake for 12 minutes, or until bread shrinks from sides of pan. Let cool in pan; cut in 4-4 1/2 inch slices. Reheat until crisp; serve.

Nancy McIntyre, GREAT FLAVORS OF LOUISIANA

CRAB LASAGNA

1/2 (16 oz.) pkg. lasagna noodles, cooked per pkg's. directions and drained
1 lb. lump crab meat
1 (10 oz.) can cream of shrimp soup
1 (8 oz.) pkg. cream cheese
1 (16 oz.) carton small curd cottage cheese
1 egg

1/2 cup onions, chopped
1/4 cup parsley, chopped
2 tsps. basil
1/2 tsp. salt
1/8 tsp. black pepper
3 fresh tomatoes, sliced
1 cup Cheddar cheese, grated

Mix crab and soup. Combine next 8 ingredients, mixing well. In greased 11x13-inch pan, layer as follows: half noodles, half crab mixture, half cheese mixture. Repeat layering once. Arrange tomatoes on top; sprinkle with grated cheese. Bake at 350°, uncovered, for 40 minutes. Remove from oven; let stand for 10 minutes. Cut into squares. MARVELOUS!! *Serves 8-10.*

Barbara Liles, Lake Charles, Louisiana

PIRATE'S PANTRY COOKBOOK, Junior League of Lake Charles

LOUISIANA FACT AND FESTIVAL:
Each year about one million people from all over the world come to Louisiana for Mardi Gras!!

The Bayou Lacombe Crab Festival is held each year in June.

MOTHER'S SEAFOOD CRAB MEAT CASSEROLE

2 large eggplant, peeled and cut
    into pieces
2 medium onions, chopped
1 green pepper, chopped
4 Tbsps. butter
2 (6 oz.) cans tomato paste
2 (6 oz.) cans water
1/2 cup green onions, chopped,
    tops and all

1/2 cup parsley, chopped
2 cloves garlic, minced
Salt and pepper to taste
Red pepper to taste
2 lbs. shrimp, shelled
1 lb. crab meat
Bread crumbs
Parmesan cheese

Saute first 3 ingredients in butter until tender. Add tomato paste and water; simmer for 5 minutes. Add next 3 ingredients. Season with salt and peppers. Cook over medium heat for 20 minutes. Add shrimp, and cook for 15 minutes more. Add crab meat; pour mixture into a buttered 13x9-inch casserole dish. Sprinkle with bread crumbs and cheese. Bake at 350° for 30 minutes. For variety, add a pint of oysters, before baking. *Serves 6-8.*

Jill Ross, West Monroe, Louisiana

LOUISIANA FESTIVALS:

Both the Old Fashioned Folk Festival in July and the Louisiana Heritage Festival in August draw folks from all around to West Monroe for great fun and marvelous food!

Mardi Gras in the Twin Cities is held in Monroe and West Monroe in March and features a festive Mardi Gras Parade and Ball!

SAUTEED SOFT SHELL CRAB

1 soft shell crab (Fresh is best.)
1 Tbsp. butter
1 garlic clove, finely chopped

Juice of 1 lemon (No substitutes!)
Enough flour in which to dredge
crab

Heat skillet until butter melts, mix garlic with melted butter, and squeeze juice from lemon directly into the pan. As butter mixture heats, dress crab by picking up flaps at edge of shell and pinching off crab's lungs with your fingers. Then, moisten crab with water by folding crab under the faucet. Put flour in shallow bowl, and dredge crab through flour until both its sides are well floured. Place crab in skillet; leave for 5-7 minutes; turn over, and cook for another 5-7 minutes. Then, enjoy! Remember, fresh crab is better, and you must use real butter. Serve hot with a glass of dry white wine. Quite Simply Delicious! Recipe is easily doubled etc.
Serves 1.

Harrell L. Griffin, Amite, Louisiana

Mr. Griffin is the Editor and Publisher of THE NEWS-DIGEST, Amite's weekly newspaper!

LOUISIANA FESTIVAL:
Amite Oyster Day is held each year in March and celebrates Louisiana's bountiful supply of fresh seafood!

MOM'S OYSTER STEW

1/2 stick butter
1-2 bunches shallots with tops
Fresh parsley to taste
2 cans celery soup
1 qt. milk

5-6 dozens oysters with juice
Salt and pepper to taste
Tabasco to taste
Lawry's or Tony's Sea Salt to taste
Paprika and parsley for garnish

Saute shallots and parsley in butter until shallots are clear. Add soup and milk; stir over low/medium heat until mixed. Add oysters, using most of juice but taking care not to have liquid too thin; cook for 10 minutes over medium high heat, stirring constantly. Milk must not scald. Continue cooking until oysters curl at edges. Add seasonings. Top with paprika and parsley. Serve with pasta salad (page 38) and garlic bread.
Serves 8-10.

Debbie Edgerton, West Monroe, Louisiana

SAUTEED OYSTERS

1/2 lb. butter, melted
3 cups oysters, liquid too
4 cloves garlic, chopped
1 cup bell pepper, chopped

1 cup mushrooms, sliced
1 tsp. pimentos, chopped
6 ozs. beer
Salt and Cayenne pepper to taste

Heat butter over medium heat; add all seasonings and vegetables; saute until done, about 5 minutes. Add oysters and beer; continue cooking until most of juice has evaporated. Serve hot over rice. WONDERFUL!!
Serves 6.

From the Recipes of Chef John Folse
THE ENCYCLOPEDIA OF CAJUN AND CREOLE CUISINE COOKBOOK

LOUISIANA PAN BROILED CATFISH FILLETS

6 catfish fillets
1 tsp. lemon pepper

1/2 cup buttermilk
Plenty of lemons, quartered

Mix seasoning with buttermilk. Marinate fillets in milk mixture for 20-30 minutes; turn twice. Heat skillet until hot; place fillets in skillet, and turn heat to medium low. When fillets become brownish, flip; brown other side. Serve immediately with lemon quarters! So good!

Nell McIntyre, Winnsboro, Louisiana

FRIED CATFISH FILLETS

1 egg, lightly beaten
1 cup milk
1/2 cup water
Salt and cayenne pepper to taste
Garlic powder to taste

1/2 cup yellow mustard
2 lbs. catfish fillets, thinly sliced
1 cup yellow corn flour
1 cup yellow corn meal
Oil for deep frying

Mix together first 5 ingredients. Place fish in milk batter. Put mustard in separate bowl. Remove fish from milk; drain well. Blend milk mixture with mustard; coat fish well in this mixture. Combine corn flour and meal. Roll fish in flour mixture until well coated. Deep fry until golden brown. Serve with Cajun Onion Rings (page 75) and Tomato Pickles (page 82). Too Good!!! Serves 4.

Chef John Folse
LAFITTE'S LANDING RESTAURANT, Donaldsonville, Louisiana

LOUISIANA FESTIVAL:
The Louisiana Catfish Festival is held in Des Allemands in July!

LOUISIANA FARM-RAISED CATFISH IN WINE SAUCE

8 medium farm-raised catfish
  fillets
1 bell pepper, chopped
6-8 green onions, chopped
4 Tbsps. butter
Soy sauce
Lemon juice (Fresh is best!)

Salt
Accent
Pepper
Worcestershire sauce
1 cup dry white wine
Fresh Parsley for garnish

Saute pepper and onion in butter; set aside. Place fillets in a lightly buttered casserole. Sprinkle fillets, lightly on each side, with next 6 ingredients. Pour vegetables over fillets. Then, pour wine over all. Bake at 350° for 30-40 minutes. Catfish will be white and flaky when done. Garnish with parsley, and serve. Delicious!! Trout and bass are so good cooked this way, but Louisiana Farm-Raised Catfish are best!! Serves 6- 8.

Adelaide Hunt, Ruston, Louisiana

LOUISIANA PLACE:
Toledo Bend, located in Sabine Parish, is home of the largest "fishing hole" in the South which has 196,000 acres of great Louisiana fishing! It is a true fisherman's delight with its abundance of black bass, striped bass, crappie, and catfish!

1½ lbs. red fish fillet
1 tsp. salt
1 tsp. pepper
½ cup water
½ cup white wine
5 Tbsps. butter
4 Tbsps. flour
1 Tbsp. green onion, chopped
½ tsp. red pepper, crushed
½ cup celery, finely chopped
¼ cup parsley, finely chopped

¼ cup juices from cooking of fish
½ cup Half and Half
¼ cup whipping cream
Salt and white pepper to taste
8 large fresh mushrooms, sliced
2 Tbsps. butter
½ cup bread crumbs, browned in 1
  Tbsp. butter
½ lb. shrimp, cooked, drained and shelled
1 doz. oysters, drained dry
¼ cup Cheddar cheese, grated

Sprinkle fish with salt and pepper. Place in shallow pan, pour water and wine around it. Bake at 400° for 15 minutes; save juices, and set aside. To make sauce, melt butter in saucepan and add flour; stir constantly until golden brown. Add next 4 ingredients; cook about 5 minutes. Add next 3 ingredients to make a thick smooth sauce. Add salt and white pepper; set aside. In separate pan, saute mushrooms in butter; drain. Place fish in an oval flat baking dish; cover with sauce. Add mushrooms, shrimp, and oysters. Sprinkle cheese over top. Sprinkle with bread crumbs. Bake at 400° until well browned and bubbling, about 15 minutes.
Serves 4 deliciously.

Julianne Lansing, New Orleans, Louisiana

119

CLE'S SALMON CAKES

1 (7 3/4 oz.) can salmon, drained
   and flaked
1/4 cup fine, dry bread crumbs
2 eggs, slightly beaten
2 Tbsps. lemon juice

1/4 tsp. pepper
Pam
1/2 cup celery, finely chopped
1/3 cup green onions, finely
   chopped, tops and all

Combine first 5 ingredients; set aside. Coat skillet with Pam; place over medium heat until hot. Add celery and onions; saute until tender. Add vegetables to salmon; mix well. Coat skillet again with Pam; place over medium high heat until hot. Shape patties, using quarter cup of mixture for each. Cook in skillet for about 2 minutes or until browned on each side.

MUSTARD SAUCE FOR SALMON CAKES

2 Tbsps. margarine, melted
1 1/2 Tbsps. all purpose flour
1 cup skim milk

1 tsp. mustard
1 tsp. lemon juice
1/4 tsp. salt

Add flour to margarine over low heat; stir until smooth. Cook for a minute; stir constantly. Gradually, add milk; cook over medium heat; stir until thickened and bubbly. Remove from heat; stir in remaining ingredients.

"This is a favorite recipe of my daughter and her family. When I visit them, I always leave a batch frozen in the freezer for them to enjoy later!"

Cleo Taylor, Jena, Louisiana

LOUISIANA FESTIVAL:
The La Salle Parish Fair is held in Jena in September.

DESSERTS

A DREAM OF A PEACHES 'N CREAM CAKE

1 box butter batter cake mix
4 cups peaches, peeled and sliced
1/2 cup water
1 1/4 cups sugar

4 Tbsps. cornstarch
1 carton sour cream
1 pt. whipping cream, whipped

Make cake per package's directions; bake in 2 pans. Cool cake; split each layer in half, making 4 layers. Cook peaches with next 3 ingredients until thick. Cool peaches until <u>very</u> cool. Place 1/3 of the peach mixture on bottom layer, cover with 1/3 of the sour cream; repeat layering twice. Ice top and sides with whipped cream. Chill. Fantastic!!

Suzanne Reed, Ruston Louisiana

BANANA NUT CAKE

1 3/4 cups butter, softened
2 1/2 cups sugar
2 eggs
1/4 tsp. salt
3/4 tsp. soda

6 Tbsps. buttermilk
1 cup <u>really ripe</u> bananas, mashed
3 cups flour
2 cups nuts, chopped

Cream sugar with butter. Add eggs, beating well.   Add salt and soda to milk; add to creamed mixture alternately with flour, mixing well after each addition. Add bananas and nuts, gently blending. Pour batter into greased Bundt or tube pan; bake for 1 1/4 hours at 325°. Quick, easy, and good!

Virginia McIntyre, Delhi, Louisiana

LOUISIANA FESTIVAL:
The Poverty Point Festival is celebrated in Delhi in October.

CAJUN CAKE

1 (15¼ oz.) can crushed pineapple,
   drained reserving ½ cup juice
⅓ cup butter or margarine, softened
1½ cups sugar
2 eggs
2 cups all purpose flour
2 tsps. baking powder
½ tsp. baking soda
¼ tsp. salt

¼ cup butter or margarine
½ cup sugar
⅓ cup evaporated milk
¼ cup flaked coconut
½ cup pecans, chopped
½ tsp. vanilla extract
Flaked coconut, toasted (optional)
Pineapple slices (optional)
Fresh pineapple leaves (optional)

Cream half cup butter with sugar using electric mixer on medium speed. Add eggs, one at a time, beating well after each addition. Combine next 4 ingredients; add to creamed mixture, alternately with reserved juice, beginning and ending with flour mixture. Mix just until blended after each addition. Stir in crushed pineapple. Pour batter into a greased and floured 10-inch Bundt pan; bake at 350° for 50-55 minutes or tests done. Cool for 10 minutes, remove from pan, and place on serving plate. Combine ¼ cup butter and next 4 ingredients in a small saucepan. Bring to boil; reduce heat, and simmer 3 minutes. Stir in vanilla, and spoon on top of warm cake. Cool. If desired, sprinkle with toasted coconut, and garnish with pineapple slices and leaves.

Jean Hurley, Lafayette, Louisiana

LOUISIANA FESTIVAL:
Festivals Acadiens, in September in Lafayette, features the best in all types of Cajun music, a food festival, crafts, and wonderful folk life segments.

CREOLE CHOCOLATE CAKE

1½ cups strong perked coffee
6 squares chocolate
4 cups cake flour, sifted
1½ tsps. baking soda
1 tsp. baking powder
1 tsp. salt

1 cup butter
2½ tsps. vanilla
3 cups brown sugar, packed firmly
4 eggs, well beaten
⅔ cup buttermilk

In top of double boiler, melt chocolate and coffee together; cool. Sift next 4 ingredients together. Cream butter and vanilla; add sugar slowly, making sure butter remains creamy. Add eggs slowly. Alternately, add dry ingredients and buttermilk to creamed mixture, beginning and ending with dry ingredients. Beat until batter is smooth. Pour batter into 2 greased and floured 8-inch cake pans or a Bundt pan; bake at 375° for 30-35 minutes or until toothpick inserted comes out clean. Use frosting below.

Suzie Stephens, Native of New Orleans, Louisiana

HOMEMADE CHOCOLATE FUDGE FROSTING

½ cup cocoa
2 cups sugar

⅔ cup milk
1 stick butter

1 tsp. vanilla

Blend together well cocoa, sugar, and milk. Boil mixture for 4 minutes. Remove from burner; stir butter into hot mixture. Cool; add vanilla. Stir until darkens and thickens. Frost cake quickly before frosting hardens.

Callie Parkman, Ruston, Louisiana

DEEP SOUTH CARROT CAKE

2 cups sugar
1½ cups Wesson oil
4 eggs
2 cups flour
2 Tbsps. cinnamon
2 Tbsps. baking powder

1 tsp. baking soda
1 tsp. nutmeg
½ tsp. salt
3 cups carrots, grated
1 cup pecans, chopped

Cream sugar and oil; add eggs, one at a time; beat well. Sift together next 6 ingredients. Slowly add dry ingredients to sugar mixture, beating well. When well blended, add carrots and nuts, mixing well. Pour batter into a greased and floured 9x13x2-inch pan. Bake at 350° for 40 minutes or tests done. Top with Best Icing.

BEST ICING

½ stick margarine, melted
1 lb. box powdered sugar

1 (8 oz.) pkg. Philadelphia Cream Cheese
2 tsps. vanilla

Cream all ingredients; ice top of cooled cake. Cover cake; refrigerate.

"This cake is my husband's favorite and not only is it delicious, it is also nutritious!!"

Kathy Steed, Shreveport, Louisiana

LOUISIANA FACT:
During the Civil War, Shreveport was for a time capital of the Trans-Mississippi Confederacy and was the <u>last</u> *city in the Confederacy to lower the Confederate flag!!*

DELUXE POUND CAKE

2 sticks margarine, at room
  temperature
3 cups sugar
1 tsp. coconut flavoring
3 cups flour
1/2 tsp. salt

1/2 cup Crisco, at room temperature
5 whole eggs
1 tsp. rum flavoring
1 tsp. baking powder
1 cup milk

Cream margarine and Crisco with sugar until fluffy. Add eggs, one at a time; mix. Combine flour, salt, and baking powder; mix. Add dry mixture, alternately with milk, to creamed mixture, begin and end with dry mixture. Add flavorings. Pour into greased and floured tube or Bundt pan; bake at 325-350° for 1 hour or tests done.

Genola Caldwell, Bernice, Louisiana

CREAM CHEESE POUND CAKE

1 (8 oz.) pkg. cream cheese
1 stick butter
2 sticks margarine
6 large eggs

3 cups sugar
3 cups plain flour
1 1/2 tsps. vanilla

Cream first 3 ingredients; add sugar; beat. Alternately, add flour and eggs to creamed mixture, blending after each addition; begin and end with flour. Add vanilla. Pour into greased and floured tube pan; bake at 300° for 1 1/2 hours or until tests done. Delicious with ice cream or your favorite sauce.

"I have tried many cakes, and I always return to this standby, my favorite!"

Claudia Cook, Urania, Louisiana

LEMON FRUIT CAKE

1 lb. butter (No substitutes!)
4 cups flour
2 cups sugar
4 cups pecans, coarsely chopped

1 box bleached (yellow) raisins
6 eggs
1 tsp. baking powder
2 ozs. _real_ lemon extract

Cream butter and sugar. Add eggs, one at a time, mixing after each addition. Mix pecans and raisins with 1 cup flour. Combine remaining flour and baking powder; alternately add flour and pecan mixtures to creamed mixture, mixing well after each addition. Add extract. Pour into 2 regular greased loaf pans; bake at 225° for 3–4 hours. So Good and Unique!!!

"I bake these cakes at Christmas time and give them as gifts!!

Linda White, Natchitoches, Louisiana

MARVELOUS APPLE-N-CRANBERRY CAKE

1 cup vegetable oil
2 cups sugar
3 eggs
3 cups flour
1 tsp. soda
1/2 tsp. salt

1 tsp. cinnamon
2-4 cups whole cranberries
2 cups apple, chopped
1 cup nuts, chopped
1 tsp. vanilla

Beat oil, sugar, and eggs together. Combine dry ingredients; stir into oil mixture. Add remaining ingredients;mix well. (Dough will be stiff.) Pour into lightly greased Bundt pan, and bake at 325° for an hour. Delicious!!

Jo Tatum Dubach Louisiana

OLD FASHIONED TEA CAKES

1 cup butter, softened
2 cups sugar
3 eggs
2 Tbsps. buttermilk

4-5 cups all purpose flour
1/2 tsp. lemon extract
2 Tbsps. baking powder

Mix all ingredients together; cover; chill overnight. Roll out thinly; cut with 3-inch cake cutter. Bake at 400° for 8-10 minutes. Serve with Old Fashioned Lemon Sauce (page 129) or Strawberry Preserves (page 79).
Yields 4-5 dozen.
"This recipe is over 100 years old. My grandmother used to make these marvelous tea cakes when I was a child!"

Lucy Roberts, Lecompte, Louisiana

RUM CAKE

1 box Duncan Hines Yellow Cake Mix
1 pkg. Jello Instant Vanilla Pudding
4 eggs
1/2 cup cold water

1/2 cup Wesson oil
1/2 cup dark rum
1 cup pecans, chopped

Combine all ingredients; mix until batter is smooth. Pour into greased and floured Bundt pan. Bake at 325° for 1 1/4 hours. Top with Delicious Glaze.

DELICIOUS GLAZE

1/4 lb. butter   1/4 cup water   1 cup sugar   1/2 cup dark rum

Combine first 3 ingredients; bring to boil. Stir for 5 minutes. Remove mixture from stove; add rum. While cake is warm, remove from Bundt pan; punch holes in with toothpicks. Drizzle glaze over cake's top and sides.

Margaret Ann James, Ruston, Louisiana

SCRUMPTIOUS GINGERBREAD

2 1/2 cups flour
1 1/2 tsps. soda (scant)
1/2 tsp. cloves
1 tsp. cinnamon
1 tsp. ginger

1/2 cup shortening
1/2 cup sugar
1 egg
1 cup Karo syrup
1 cup hot water

Sift first five ingredients together. Cream shortening and sugar; add egg, and beat in syrup. Beat together alternately the flour mixture and hot water with creamed mixture. Bake at 350° in greased 9x13-inch pan for 25-30 minutes. Serve warm topped with Old Fashioned Lemon Sauce.

OLD FASHIONED LEMON SAUCE

1 cup sugar
1 egg, beaten
1 stick butter, softened

1/4 cup water
3 Tbsps. fresh lemon juice
Rind of 1 lemon, grated

In saucepan, combine all ingredients; mix well. Cook over medium heat, stirring constantly until mixture boils. Serve warm over gingerbread. Yields 1 1/3 cups.

Carolyn McGraw, Alexandria, Louisiana

LOUISIANA PLACE:
Nottoway Plantation, located near White Castle (18 miles south of Baton Rouge) is the South's largest plantation home. Nottoway, truly an American castle, has 64 rooms with over 53,000 square feet of living space! Completed in 1859, Nottoway, designed by Henry Howard, is a lovely blend of the Greek Revival and Italianate architectural styles.

STRAWBERRY JAM CAKE

1 cup butter, softened
1/2 cup sugar
1 cup strawberry jam
1/2 cup strong black coffee
1 tsp. cinnamon

1/4 tsp. ground cloves
3 eggs, separated
2 1/2 cups flour
1 tsp. baking soda
4 Tbsps. sour cream

Cream butter with sugar, beating well. Combine next 4 ingredients; add to creamed mixture. Beat egg yolks; add to jam mixture. Dissolve soda in sour cream. Alternately add flour and sour cream mixture to jam mixture, mixing well each time. Beat egg whites until stiff. Fold whites into jam mixture. Bake in cake pans at 350° for 45-50 minutes or until tests done. Let cool and ice with Best Brown Sugar Icing. Wonderful!!

BEST BROWN SUGAR ICING

3 egg whites
1/3 cup light Karo syrup
2 cups light brown sugar
2 Tbsps. water

1/4 tsp. cream of tartar
Pinch of salt
1 tsp. vanilla
1 Tbsp. brown sugar

Combine first 6 ingredients in top of double boiler over rapidly boiling water; cook beating continually, for 6-8 minutes. Remove from heat, add vanilla, and beat until mixture is thick enough to spread. Frost cooled cake; then, sprinkle tablespoon of sugar around top of cake.

OLD SOUTHERN SECRETS COOKBOOK, GEMS OF ANTE-BELLUM DAYS

BEST HOMEMADE ICE CREAM

6 eggs, whipped
1 1/3 cups sugar
1/2 pt. whipping cream
1/2 tsp. salt
1/2 gallon milk
2 tsps. vanilla

In a saucepan, combine first 5 ingredients. In top of double boiler, heat mixture until it coats a spoon. Cool; add vanilla. Freeze in ice cream freezer, according to freezer's directions. Then, enjoy!

"For a wonderful Peach Ice Cream, use this recipe, and add 2 cups mashed peaches and use only 1 teaspoon of vanilla. Delicious!"

Callie Parkman, Ruston, Louisiana

EASY CHOCOLATE ICE CREAM

2 (14 oz.) cans Eagle Brand milk
2 cans evaporated milk
1 (16 oz.) can chocolate syrup
Milk (regular sweet)

Mix first 3 ingredients together. Finish filling up ice cream freezer with milk. Make per freezer's instructions.
Yields 1 1/2 quarts.

Glenda Fuller, Dubach, Louisiana

LOUISIANA NOTABLE:
Truman Capote, born in New Orleans, devoted himself to writing and living an artistic life. His works include his highly acclaimed first novel, OTHER VOICES, OTHER ROOMS, BREAKFAST AT TIFFANY'S, A CHRISTMAS MEMORY, and his "nonfiction novel," IN COLD BLOOD which is about the 1959 murder of a Kansas family.

FROZEN CREOLE CREAM CHEESE

12 ozs. large curd cottage cheese	¾ cup sugar
2 cups Half and Half	6 Tbsps. fresh lemon juice, strained
1 cup whipping cream	1 tsp. vanilla

Blend cottage cheese and 1 cup Half and Half in blender or food processor until mixture is smooth. Add another cup Half and Half, whipping cream, sugar, lemon juice, and vanilla. Mix until smooth. Transfer to ice cream maker, and process according to manufacturer's instructions; finished texture will be light and creamy. Serve immediately with fig conserve (page 79), or freeze until ready to serve. TRULY A LOUISIANA TREAT!! Serves 10.

Julianne Lansing, New Orleans, Louisiana

Julianne, her home, and cooking (including this recipe) were featured in the March, 1987, edition of BON APPETIT. This delightful recipe was served to end a magnificent meal that she and her husband, Paul, had served their guests during an annual Mardi Gras celebration!

LOUISIANA FACT:
The St. Charles Avenue Streetcar Line, in New Orleans, is one of the last operative streetcar lines in the United States and provides a memorable ride past the antebellum homes of the beautiful and famous Garden District.

FIG ICE CREAM

2 (17 oz.) cans Kadota figs, drained
1 cup milk
1¾ cups sugar, divided
2 Tbsps. lemon juice
1½ Tbsps. creme de cacao
2 eggs, beaten
3 cups milk
2 cups whipping cream

Combine figs, 1 cup milk, 1 cup sugar, lemon juice, and creme de caccao in blender; mix until pureed. In large bowl, combine eggs, puree, remaining sugar, 3 cups milk, and whipping cream;. Freeze in 4-quart ice cream freezer per freezer's instructions. Let ice cream ripen for an hour. Fantastic!! *Yields 3 quarts.*

Jean Hurley, Lafayette, Louisiana

MOMMA BOOTH'S STRAWBERRY ICE CREAM

1 (14 oz.) can Eagle Brand Milk
1 large can Pet Milk
1½ cups sugar
6 eggs
1 tsp. vanilla
Strawberries, fresh or frozen, and
   to taste
Milk (regular sweet)

Combine first 5 ingredients. Separately, sweeten strawberries with additional sugar to taste; mash. Add strawberries to milk mixture, stirring well. Pour mixture into an ice cream freezer, and add milk to "fill line." Freeze per freezer's directions. So Southern!! *Serves 6-8.*

Kathy Booth, Shreveport, Louisiana

LOUISIANA FESTIVAL:
The Louisiana State Fair is held annually in Shreveport in October and provides an encompassing depiction of Louisiana's commerce, industry, and agriculture. It is one of the ten largest state fairs in the United States!

A TREAT OF A CARROT PUDDING

2 Tbsps. butter
1 cup sugar
2 eggs
1½ cups raw carrots, grated
¼ tsp. ground cloves
½ tsp. cinnamon
¼ tsp. nutmeg

¼ tsp. salt
1 cup, flour sifted
Grated rind of 1 lemon
Grated rind of 1 orange
1 tsp. baking soda
1 cup raw potatoes, grated
½ lb. citron, thinly sliced (optional)

Cream butter and sugar; add eggs; beat well. Add next 8 ingredients; blend well. Add soda to potatoes, stirring until soda is dissolved. Add potatoes to carrot mixture; then add citron, mixing it well through batter. Butter large mold and place sheet of greased wax paper on bottom of mold; pour in pudding. Cover mold, and place in pot of boiling water; steam for 2 hours. Serve with generous topping of heavy or whipped cream. At Christmas or Thanksgiving, top whipped cream and/or hot mincemeat.
Serves 6-8.

OLD SOUTHERN SECRETS COOKBOOK, GEMS OF ANTE-BELLUM DAYS

LOUISIANA NOTABLE:

Shirley Ann Grau, the noted novelist, was born and resides in New Orleans. Her first book, THE BLACK PRINCE AND OTHER STORIES, a collection of stories about the people from bayou country, received wide critical acclaim and her novel, THE KEEPER OF THE HOUSE, won a Pulitzer Price. Her works include THE HARD BLUE SKY, and THE CONDOR PASSES.

RICE PUDDING, LOUISIANA STYLE

1/2 cup washed, uncooked rice
4 cups milk
1/2 cup molasses
1/2 tsp. cinnamon
1/2 tsp. nutmeg

1/2 tsp. salt
1/2 cup golden raisins
1 Tbsp. butter
Whipped cream

Combine, and mix well first 7 ingredients. Pour into a 2-quart casserole that has been greased with butter. Bake at 300° for 2 hours; stir every 15 minutes. Top with tablespoon of butter for the last 15 minutes of cooking time. Serve warm topped with heavy cream. WONDERFUL AND EASY! Serves 6.

FRENCH CREAM

1 cup heavy cream, whipped
1 cup powdered sugar, sifted
1 cup sour cream
1/2 tsp. fresh lemon rind, grated
1 oz. orange liqueur

2 pts. strawberries _or_ peaches _or_
    blueberries _or_ raspberries _or_ a
    combination thereof
Grated chocolate

Fold into whipped cream the sugar, sour cream, and rind; then add liqueur. Arrange fresh fruit in a pretty see through bowl. Spoon cream over fruit. Garnish with chocolate. A Pretty Delight!!

NIBBLES COOKS CAJUN COOKBOOK

LOUISIANA FACT:
The Konriko Rice Mill and Company Store, located in New Iberia, is the oldest operated rice mill in the United States.

TRAMMEL'S SOUTHERN BREAD PUDDING

8 slices thinly sliced bread, toasted
   on both sides and crumbled into
   small pieces
2 sticks butter, melted
4 eggs
2 cups sugar

4 cups milk
1/2 tsp. cinnamon
1/2 tsp. nutmeg
1/2 cup raisins
1-2 tsps. vanilla extract

Put toast into pyrex baking dish. Pour butter over crumbs. Beat together eggs and sugar; add milk and spices. Pour milk mixture over crumbs; let stand until crumbs absorb some of mixture. Stir in raisins and extract. Bake at 350° for an hour or until pudding is light brown and set in middle. *Serves 8-12.*

> *"When we have something at church, this is always a request!!"*
>
> Liz Trammel. Dubach, Louisiana

BANANAS LAFOURCHE

4 bananas, sliced in half and
   lengthwise
1 stick butter

3/4 cup light brown sugar
1/2 tsp. cinnamon
1/2 cup banana liqueur

Melt butter over medium heat. Add sugar and cinnamon; dissolve. Cook sugar for 5 minutes; turn once. Add bananas; cook until tender, about 2 minutes. Add liqueur; ignite; as flame dies, stir. Serve warm over ice cream. *Serves 4.*

John S. Walther, Thibodaux, Louisiana

EASY 'N GOOD PECAN MERINGUE BROWNIES

1 stick butter or margarine, softened	1/2 tsp. salt
1 cup sugar	1 cup chocolate chips (optional)
1 tsp. vanilla	1 tsp. baking powder
2 eggs	3/4 cup brown sugar
1 1/2 cups flour	1 cup pecans (chopped, if desired)

Cream butter and sugar; add vanilla. Separate 1 egg, and put egg white aside. Combine 1 egg and yolk with sugar mixture; mix well. Mix in flour, salt, and baking powder; beat well. Add chocolate chips. Spread mixture into greased 9x13-inch pan. Whip egg white until just stiff; beat in brown sugar. Fold in pecans. Carefully spread pecan mixture over top of batter. Bake at 300° for 30 minutes. Cool, and cut into squares. YUM! With chocolate chips, YUM, YUM!!

Gwen McKee, Native of Baton Rouge, Louisiana

Gwen McKee is director of her own publishing company, Quail Ridge Press, and produces a line of cookbooks which includes BEST OF THE BEST OF LOUISIANA!

LOUISIANA NOTABLE:
Huey Long, the famous Louisiana governor, was born in 1893 near Winnfield. He served as Louisiana's governor and later as a United States senator. Long was so powerful that in Louisiana he was known as the "Kingfish."

MRS. GREEN'S HEAVENLY PRALINE DELIGHTS

4 eggs
1 box brown sugar
1½ cups flour
1½ tsps. baking powder

1 tsp. vanilla
Pinch of salt
2 cups pecans, chopped

Mix well first 6 ingredients; cook in top of double boiler until mixture is really hot, about 15 minutes. Add pecans. Pour mixture into greased 9x13-inch pan; bake at 325° for 20 minutes. Let cool; cut into squares.

FAVORITE BROWNIES

1 cup butter
2 cups sugar
4 eggs
1½ cups flour

½ tsp. baking powder
¼ cup cocoa
1 tsp. vanilla
1½ cups pecans, chopped

Combine all ingredients together, mixing well. Pour into greased 9x13-inch pan; bake at 400° for 15 minutes. Don't over cook! Delicious and Easy!

Elaine Edwards, Currently Louisiana's First Lady

LOUISIANA FESTIVAL:
Enjoy performances of the world's greatest playwright during the Louisiana Shakespeare Festival in Lake Charles the last weekend in July and the first weekend in August!

JENNIE'S FROSTED NUTMEG LOGS

1 cup butter, softened
3/4 cup sugar
1 egg
3 cups all purpose flour

1-1 1/4 tsps. ground nutmeg
2 tsps. rum extract
2 tsps. vanilla extract
Ground nutmeg for cookie tops

Cream butter, gradually adding sugar and beating until fluffy. Add egg. Combine flour and nutmeg; add to creamed mixture. Stir in extracts. Shape dough into 3x1/2-inch logs, place 2 inches apart on cookie sheets, and bake at 350° for 12 minutes or until lightly browned. Cool. Frost; run fork tines lengthwise across frosting on each; top with nutmeg.
Yields 4 1/2 dozen.

VANILLA–RUM FROSTING

1/2 cup butter, softened
3 cups powdered sugar, sifted and
   divided into 2 equal parts

2 Tbsps. Half and Half or milk
1 tsp. vanilla extract
1 tsp. rum extract

Cream butter, gradually adding half the sugar. Add remaining ingredients; beat until smooth.
Yields 1 1/2 cups.

"These cookies can be made ahead and frozen in a container with waxed paper between the layers. Let them sit out until thawed before opening. They're just like fresh baked!"

Kathleen Drott, Pineville, Louisiana

ROYAL OATMEAL COOKIES

1 cup shortening
1 stick butter
1 cup white sugar
1 cup brown sugar
2 eggs
2 cups flour
1 tsp. baking powder
1 1/2 tsps. soda

1/2 tsp. salt
2 cups corn flakes
1 cup coconut
1 cup pecans
2 cups oatmeal, uncooked
1 tsp. vanilla
1 (6 oz.) pkg. semi-sweet
    chocolate chips

In large bowl, cream sugars, shortening, and butter. Add eggs one at a time. Sift together flour, baking powder and soda, and salt. Add to creamed mixture. Add remaining ingredients; gently mix. Shape in balls, and place on greased cookie sheet. Bake at 350° for 12 minutes. TOO GOOD!! FIT FOR A KING!!!
Yields 5 dozen.

Nancy McIntyre, GREAT FLAVORS OF LOUISIANA

LOUISIANA PLACE:
The oldest Catholic cathedral, still actively used in the United States, is the St. Louis Cathedral, located in New Orleans' French Quarter. This majestic edifice was built in 1794.

6 Tbsps. butter (No substitutes!)
1 (14 oz.) can Eagle Brand milk
1 (12 oz.) pkg. chocolate chips

1 cup flour, rounded
1 (5½-6 oz.) pkg. chocolate chips

In saucepan over medium heat, whip together first 3 ingredients. When chocolate is melted and mixture is well blended, remove from burner; add flour; cool. Stir in remaining chips; let mixture "sit" a few minutes. Drop batter, a spoonful at a time, onto greased cookie sheet. Cook at 300° for 6-7 minutes or until each cookie is firm, but still gooey.
Yields 3 dozen cookies.

Ellen Reynolds, GREAT FLAVORS OF LOUISIANA

MILAN'S POTATO CHIP COOKIES

½ lb. butter, softened
½ cup sugar
2 cups flour, sifted
½ cup walnuts, chopped

½ cup potato chips, crumbed
1 tsp. vanilla
Powdered sugar

Cream butter and sugar. Combine nuts and chips; add flour and vanilla; mix with creamed mixture. Roll dough into small balls; flatten with fingers on ungreased cookie sheet. Bake at 350° for 20 minutes. (These cookies should not be browned.) While warm, dust with powdered sugar.
Yields about 3 dozen marvelous cookies!

Polly Schmitz, Native of Baton Rouge, Louisiana

CHOCOLATE PRALINES

7 cups whipping cream
4 cups sugar
1½ cups pecan pieces

2½ Tbsps. unsweetened cocoa
powder, sifted

In saucepan over low heat, cook cream and sugar, swirling pan occasionally until sugar dissolves. Bring to boil. Reduce heat to medium; cook until candy thermometer registers 240°F. (soft ball stage), about 50 minutes; do not stir. Mix in pecans; remove from heat. Stir 5 minutes to cool. Mix in cocoa; spoon mixture onto waxed paper by tablespoons. Cool completely. Store in airtight container; do not refrigerate. Wonderful and Special!! *Yields about 5 dozen.*

Chef Gerard Maras
MR. B'S BISTRO, New Orleans, Louisiana

CINDY'S BEST PEANUT BUTTER FUDGE

2 (12 oz.) bags butterscotch morsels
1 (28 oz.) jar crunchy peanut butter

2 (14 oz.) cans condensed milk

Melt first 2 ingredients over medium heat, stirring often. Do not scorch! When all melted, remove from stove; stir in milk. Mix well. Spray 13x9-inch pan with Pam; pour in mixture. Refrigerate until firm. OUTSTANDING!! *Makes 100 1-inch squares.*

Cindy Moore, Lake Charles, Louisiana
PIRATE'S PANTRY COOKBOOK, Junior League of Lake Charles

MAMA'S PEANUT BRITTLE

2 cups raw peanuts
1 cup white Karo syrup

1 cup sugar
1 tsp. baking soda

In pot with same circumference as burner, mix together sugar, syrup, and peanuts. Cook mixture for 20 minutes over medium heat. Syrup will turn color of brandy at end of cooking time. Grease well 2 platters; set aside. Add soda to peanut mixture; stir rapidly to mix. Put mixture on platters. Let cool; turn as mixture cools. Break into small pieces.
Yields about 20 small pieces.

Anne Lott-Doughty, Zenoria, Louisiana

NOON'S PRALINES

1 stick butter
1 large can evaporated milk
3 cups sugar

3 cups pecans
1 tsp. vanilla

In heavy pot over low heat, combine first 3 ingredients. Stir often. Cook until soft ball stage (small amount forms ball when dropped into water), 240° on candy thermometer. Add pecans; cook until mixture forms medium sized ball. Remove from heat, add vanilla, and stir until mixture sticks around edge of pot. Drop mixture by spoonfuls onto waxed paper. Cool.
Yields about 3½ dozen.

Ethel Deloge, Baton Rouge, Louisiana

LOUISIANA FESTIVAL:
The Louisiana Praline Festival is held in Houma in May.

CHOCOLATE MOUSSE PIE

CRUST:

3 cups chocolate wafer crumbs   *1 stick unsalted butter, melted*

Combine crumbs and butter. Firmly press on bottom and completely up sides of 10-inch spring form pan. Chill for 30 minutes.

MOUSSE FILLING:

1 lb. semisweet chocolate   *2 cups whipping cream*
2 eggs   *6 Tbsps. powdered sugar*
4 egg yolks   *4 egg whites, at room temperature*

Soften chocolate in top of double boiler. Let cool to lukewarm. Add whole eggs; mix. Add yolks; mix until well blended. Whip cream with sugar until soft peaks form. Beat egg whites until stiff. Stir a little whipped cream and whites into chocolate mixture to lighten. Fold in remaining cream and whites. Pour mixture into crust; chill at least 6 hours.

TOPPING:

1-1½ cups whipping cream   *1 Tbsp. chocolate wafer crumbs*
2 Tbsps. powdered sugar

Whip cream and sugar until soft peaks form. Loosen pie crust with knife; remove spring form. Spread topping over filling; sprinkle with crumbs.

"This is always a hit at dinner parties and on special occasions and has become my oldest son's birthday cake!!"

Nina Long, Alexandria, Louisiana

MARTHA'S CHOCOLATE PEANUT BUTTER PIE

4 eggs
1 cup dark corn syrup
3/4 cup sugar
1/2 cup +1 Tbsp. peanut butter
1 1/2 tsps. vanilla

3/4 cup salted peanuts
1-1 1/2 cups semi-sweet chocolate
    chips
1 graham cracker crust <u>or</u> 1 9-inch
    unbaked pie shell

Preheat oven to 400°. With electric mixer, beat first 5 ingredients until smooth. Stir in peanuts. Sprinkle pie shell with chips; pour in peanut mixture. Bake for 15 minutes. Reduce oven to 350°; continue baking for 30 minutes or until fork inserted in center comes out clean. Fantastic!!

SOUTHERN LEMON CHESS PIE

2 cups sugar
1 Tbsp. flour
1 Tbsp. corn meal
4 eggs, unbeaten
1/2 cup margarine

1/4 cup milk
1/4 cup lemon juice
1 lemon rind, grated
1 9-inch pie shell, unbaked

Mix first 3 ingredients together. Combine sugar mixture with remaining ingredients; mix well. Pour into pie shell; bake at 450° for 10 minutes. Reduce heat to 350°; bake for 25 minutes more. MARVELOUS!

Joanna Steed, Ruston, Louisiana

LOUISIANA FESTIVAL:
The Northeast Louisiana Cotton Festival and Fair is held in Bastrop in September.

NO FUSS-NO CRUST COCONUT PIE

2 cups milk
3/4 cup sugar
1/2 cup biscuit mix
4 eggs

1/4 cup margarine
1 1/2 tsps. vanilla
1 cup coconut

Combine first 6 ingredients in blender; blend on low for 3 minutes. Pour into greased 9-inch pie pan. Let stand for 5 minutes. Sprinkle with coconut; bake at 350° for 40 minutes.
Serves 6-8.

Carolyn Eakin, Lake Charles, Louisiana

PERFECT PEACH PIE

1 (8 oz.)container Cool Whip
1 (14 oz.) can condensed milk
1/2 cup lemon juice

6 fresh peaches, peeled and sliced
1 graham cracker crust (page 152)

Mix together first 3 ingredients; stir in peaches. Pour into crust; refrigerate until firm. DELICIOUS!!
Serves 8.

"You may use strawberries instead of peaches. Wonderful!"

Nadine McCall, Lake Charles, Louisiana

PIRATE'S PANTRY COOKBOOK, Junior League of Lake Charles

LOUISIANA FACT:
Louisiana's state flower is the magnolia. Its state bird is the Brown Pelican.

BEST OF ALL COFFEE ICE CREAM PIE

1 (8 oz.) pkg. Nabisco Famous
   Chocolate Wafers; crumbled
1 stick butter, melted
1/2 cup pecans, finely chopped
1 qt. coffee ice cream, softened

2 cups whipping cream
3 Tbsps. sugar
1 Tbsp. Irish whiskey (optional)
1-2 tsps. instant espresso coffee
   (optional)

Preheat oven to 350°. Mix crumbs with butter and pecans. Firmly press mixture into 9-inch pie plate. Bake for 8 minutes or until set. Cool crust; freeze for an hour. Fold in ice cream, spreading about evenly. Cover with plastic wrap; freeze until ice cream is set. Whip cream into soft peaks; add sugar, whiskey, and 1 teaspoon coffee. Swirl whipped cream over ice cream, and sprinkle a teaspoon of coffee over topping. You may substitute Cool Whip for whipped cream. TRULY THE BEST OF ALL!! EASY TOO!!

Carol Colclough Strickland, Native of New Orleans, Louisiana

LOUISIANA NOTABLE:
Robert Rucker, born in New Orleans, now makes his home in Covington. Mr. Rucker, a popular Louisiana artist, paints steamboats, plantation homes, and rural scenes. He has said that he is afraid these places which depict Louisiana's past will disappear and feels that his paintings will help preserve the images for future generations.

OLD FASHIONED SOUTHERN LEMON PIE

3 egg yolks
1 whole egg
1¼ cups sugar
⅛ tsp. salt
5 Tbsps. bread flour

¾ cup boiling water
½ tsp. lemon rind, grated
¼ cup lemon juice (Fresh is best!)
1 Tbsp. butter
1 9-inch pie shell, baked

Beat together egg yolks and whole egg until light. Gradually, add cup of sugar. Combine remaining sugar with salt and flour; add to egg mixture. Beat until well blended. Gradually, pour boiling water over mixture, stirring constantly. Add lemon rind and juice. Cook in top part of double boiler until is thick, about 30 minutes; stir occasionally. Add butter; remove from burner. Cool slightly, pour into pie shell; top with meringue.

DIVINE PIE MERINGUE

3 egg whites, beaten until stiff   ½ cup sugar   ½ tsp. vinegar

Gradually add sugar to whites; continue beating until sugar dissolves. Add vinegar; beat. Pile meringue on top of lemon filling, spread in swirls, making sure meringue touches pastry. Preheat oven to 300°; bake meringue until golden brown, about 12-18 minutes.

Callie Ratcliff, St. Joseph, Louisiana

LOUISIANA PLACE:
The Destrehan Plantation, the closest East Bank plantation to New Orleans, was built in 1787 and is the oldest plantation home remaining in the lower Mississippi River Valley.

OLD FASHIONED PEACH COBBLER

2 1/2 cups ripe peaches, sliced
1 cup sugar
1 1/2 cups plain flour
Pinch of salt

1/2 cup butter flavored Crisco
6 tsps. iced water
Butter
Sugar

Combine peaches and sugar; pour into pyrex dish. Mix next 4 ingredients until "doughy." Roll out pastry, cut into strips, and place over peaches. Dot pastry with butter; sprinkle with sugar. Bake at 450° until pastry is brown.
Serves 6-8.

PECAN RITZ PIE

20 Ritz crackers, crumbled
1 scant tsp. baking powder
3 egg whites
1 1/2 -2 cups sugar

1 cup pecans, chopped
1/2 pt. whipping cream, whipped
  with 1-2 tsps. sugar

Beat egg whites and baking soda together until stiff. Add sugar gradually, beating thoroughly. Fold in nuts and cracker crumbs. Bake for 20 minutes at 350° in greased 9-inch pie pan. Cool; top with whipped cream.

Joanna Steed, Ruston, Louisiana

LOUISIANA PLACE AND FESTIVAL:
Ruston, nestled in North Louisiana's Piney Hills country, is the Peach Capital of Louisiana and home of the Louisiana Peach Festival each June.

AUNT LETHA'S PECAN PIE

8 Tbsps. sugar
2 cups milk, scalded
1 cup sugar
1/4 tsp. salt
1/2 tsp. vanilla
4 Tbsps. flour

4 egg yolks, beaten
1 9-inch pie shell, unbaked
1 1/2 cups pecans, chopped
4 egg whites
8 Tbsps. sugar
1/4 cup pecans, chopped

In heavy saucepan over low heat, melt 8 tablespoons sugar. Pour in milk; stir until combined well. Combine next 4 ingredients, mixing well; add to milk mixture. Add yolks, and blend; pour mixture into pie shell, and bake at 375° until filling is firm, about 40 minutes. Remove from oven; spread 1 1/2 cups pecans over top of filling. Make meringue by whipping into peaks egg whites and 8 tablespoons sugar. Cover pecan layer with meringue; sprinkle with quarter cup pecans. Bake at 350° until meringue is golden brown, about 15-20 minutes. MAGNIFICENT AND SO SPECIAL!!

"Melting the first 8 tablespoons of sugar takes awhile. Be certain that your saucepan is heavy with a thick bottom or put the sugar in the top of a double boiler over boiling water. Aunt Letha's pie is so special and unusual and well worth the small amount of extra preparation time!!"

Billie Taylor Gough, Native of Jena, Louisiana

LOUISIANA FESTIVAL:
The Louisiana Pecan Festival is held annually in Colfax in November.

THREE STORY DREAM PIE

CRUST:

| 1 stick margarine | 1 cup pecans, chopped | 1 cup flour |

FIRST LAYER:

| 1 cup powdered sugar | 1 tsp. vanilla |
| 1 (8 oz.) pkg. cream cheese | 1½ cups Cool Whip |

SECOND LAYER:

2 (3 oz.) pkgs. instant chocolate pudding, prepared per pkg.'s directions and combined with 1 tsp. vanilla.

THIRD LAYER:

1½ cups Cool Whip

To make crust, combine margarine and flour, mixing well; add pecans, and press into 9x9-inch pan. Bake at 350° for 20-25 minutes; cool. Cream sugar, creamed cheese, and vanilla. Blend in Cool Whip. Spread over cooled crust. Spread pudding over first layer. Top with Cool Whip. May use your favorite pudding or 2 different puddings.

Iva Melancon, Sulphur, Louisiana

LOUISIANA NOTABLE:
Walker Percy, one of America's finest living novelists, has been a resident of Covington, Louisiana, for almost forty years. In 1962, he won the National Book Award for fiction for his novel, THE MOVIEGOER. Among his other works are THE LAST GENTLEMAN, LOVE IN THE RUINS, LANCELOT, and the newly published, THE THANATOS SYNDROME.

GREAT FLAVOR'S PUMPKIN ICE CREAM PIE

1/4 cup brown sugar
3/4 cup pumpkin, cooked and mashed
* (May substitute canned.)*
1/2 tsp. ginger
1/2 tsp. cinnamon
1/8 tsp. nutmeg

1/8 tsp. ground cloves
1/4 tsp. salt
1 qt. vanilla ice cream, softened
1/2 cup pecans, chopped
Whipped cream (optional)

In saucepan, combine first 7 ingredients, mixing well. Bring mixture to boil, stirring constantly; remove from stove, and let cool. Beat pumpkin mixture into ice cream; add pecans, and gently mix. Pour mixture into None Better Graham Cracker Crust. Freeze until frozen. Top individual pieces of pie with whipped cream and a couple pecan halves.

NONE BETTER GRAHAM CRACKER CRUST

3 egg whites
1 cup sugar
3/4 cup graham cracker crumbs

1/2 cup pecans, finely chopped
1 tsp. baking powder
1/2 tsp. vanilla

Beat egg whites until stiff, adding sugar gradually. Fold in remaining ingredients, mixing well. Pour mixture into greased 9-inch pie pan; bake at 350° for 35 minutes. Let cool before filling. Great with other pie fillings!!

GREAT FLAVORS OF LOUISIANA

LOUISIANA FACT:
In 1954, Louisiana's Legislature set aside April 30 of each year as Louisiana Day! This is the official date of the Louisiana Purchase in 1803 and the official date of the admission of the State of Louisiana into the Union in 1812.

For Louisianans, Lagniappe means a little gift, that something extra one gives or receives. Louisiana store owners, when a large purchase is made or a monthly bill is promptly paid, will sometimes give a little gift as Lagniappe to their customers. We hope that our "something extra," the Louisiana Roux, will stimulate you to take this Cajun and Creole base for just about any "one pot" meal and create your own marvelous recipes, Cajun and Creole style!! **THE EDITORS**

——— LOUISIANA ROUX ———

1 cup all purpose flour   *1 cup vegetable oil*

Pour oil into heavy saucepan; heat over medium heat until hot. Add flour; stir with long handled spoon until pasty and smooth. Stir constantly until brown; remove from heat. Roux should have a very nutty aroma, not smell scorched, and is the best as a thickening agent for soups, stews, etc.

"A good roux is the best foundation for all Cajun Cuisine and will be used in dishes ranging from vegetables to gravies. For all Real Louisiana Cooking, it is important to practice and master this unique base!"

From the recipes of Chef John Folse
THE ENCYCLOPEDIA OF CAJUN AND CREOLE CUISINE COOKBOOK

EDITOR'S NOTE: We are so proud to be able to share with you some of John Folse's superb recipes! Mr. Folse is internationally known, has won many awards, and has prepared his famous 'Taste of Louisiana' for the White House, the Congress, and Hollywood's top celebrities including Cybil Shepherd! He has taken his "black pots" to Moscow, Beijing, London, Paris, and New York! Craig Claiborne, the acclaimed food writer, describes Chef Folse as "one of America's foremost Cajun-Creole Chefs!"

INDEX

GREAT FLAVORS OF LOUISIANA

Post Office Box 922

Pine Bluff, Arkansas 71613

Please send_____ copies of GREAT FLAVORS OF LOUISIANA and or

_____ copies of GREAT FLAVORS OF MISSISSIPPI at

$8.30 per copy (includes postage, handling, and tax.)

Telephone your order by calling 501-536-8221.

Enclosed is my check or money order for $ _____

Name_____

Street_____

City_____ State _____ Zip_____

We, at SOUTHERN FLAVORS, INC., appreciate your patronage and request that you send us names and addresses of bookstores, gift shops, etc., in your area.

_____

_____

_____

_____

_____

_____

Thank you for taking the time to respond to our request, and please watch for other SOUTHERN FLAVORS' publications and products!!